Buddhism

Major World Religions Series

Donald K. Swearer, Editor

Buddhism

BY DONALD K. SWEARER, Ph.D

Argus Communications
Niles, Illinois 60648

ACKNOWLEDGEMENTS

Excerpt from *The Teachings of the Compassionate Buddha,* ed. by E. A. Burtt. Copyright © 1955 by The New American Library. Reprinted by permission of The New American Library.

Excerpts from *Buddhist Texts Through the Ages,* ed. by Edward Conze. Copyright © 1954 by Philosophical Library. Reprinted by permission of Philosophical Library and Faber and Faber, London.

PHOTO CREDITS

Juan V. Cadiz/TOM STACK & ASSOCIATES   cover: upper right
Denchai Photo   xix, 67
Keith Gunnar/TOM STACK & ASSOCIATES   cover: lower left
Jean-Claude LeJeune   cover; top center, upper left
Joseph C. Lowey   54 (top and bottom)
Donald K. Swearer   7, 14, 34, 43, 63, 71
Robert Wick/TOM STACK & ASSOCIATES   cover: lower right

MAPS
Homer Grooman

COVER DESIGN
Gene Tarpey

© Copyright Argus Communications 1977

Printed in the United States of America.

Argus Communications
7440 Natchez Avenue
Niles, Illinois 60648

International Standard Book Number 0-913592-96-X

Library of Congress Number 77-82794

1   2   3   4   5   6   7   8   9   0

To Nancy, whose critical revision
greatly enhanced this volume.

Contents

Foreword

"The study of religion is the study of mankind." Religion touches the deepest feelings of the human heart and is part of every human society. In modern times religion has been studied by sociologists and anthropologists as a cultural institution. Psychologists see religion as an expression of an inner human need. Philosophers view it as a system of thought or doctrine. Historians consider religion a part of the intellectual and institutional development of a given era.

What is religion? Modern definitions range from "what man does in his solitude" to "an expression of collective identity," and from "man's experience of awe and fascination before a tremendous mystery" to "projective feelings of dependency." The scope of life that religion is identified with is so vast, and the assumptions about the nature of religion are so varied, that we may readily agree with those who say that the study of religion is the study of mankind.

Religion takes many forms, or perhaps it would be better to say that there are many aspects to religion. They include *belief* (e.g., the belief in a creator God), *ritual action* (e.g., making offerings to that God), *ethical action* (following God's law), the formation of *religious communities,* and the formulation of *creeds and doctrinal systems.*

Joachim Wach, a scholar of religion, has pictured religion in terms of religious experience which expresses itself in thought, action, and fellowship.[1] In this view religion is rooted in religious experience, and all other aspects of religion are expressions of that experience. For example, the Buddha's experience of the highest Truth (in Buddhism called *Nirvana*) led him to teach what he had experienced (known as *dharma*) and resulted in the formation of a monastic community (known as *sangha*).

It must be remembered that religions develop within particular historical and cultural traditions and not in a vacuum. This fact has several profound consequences for the study of religion. In the first place it means that religion can never be completely separated from

---

[1] Joachim Wach, *The Comparative Study of Religions* (New York: Columbia University Press, 1958).

particular historical and cultural traditions. For example, early Christian thought was deeply influenced by both Semitic and Greek traditions, and such central Christian celebrations as Christmas and Easter owe their form to pre-Christian European traditions.

Furthermore, since a religion is subject to cultural and historical influences, its traditions are always developing relative to particular times and places. For example, the form of worship used in the Buddhist Churches of America (founded in the late nineteenth century) has as much or more in common with American Protestant worship services than with its traditional Japanese form. A religion, then, as part of a specific historical and cultural stream, changes through time and can be fully understood only in relationship to its historical and cultural forms. By way of generalization we might say that Christianity as a religion is only partially understood in terms of its central beliefs and that a fuller or more complete understanding demands a knowledge of its worldwide history and the influence of its various cultural traditions.

In the second place, since a religion develops within particular historical and cultural settings, it also influences its setting. In other words, there is a give-and-take relationship between a religion and its environment. For example, in traditional societies like medieval Europe, Christianity was the inspiration for much of the art and architecture. The same is true for traditional India, where Buddhism and Hinduism decisively affected artistic forms, or for traditional Persia with Islam. Of course, religion influences its environment in other than merely artistic realms. It has had profound effects on modes of behavior (ethics), conceptions of state (politics), forms of economic endeavor—indeed, on all aspects of life.

As a consequence of the pervasive influence of religion in so many aspects of human endeavor, students of religion and society have observed that in traditional societies religion was never isolated. That is, nothing within the given society was perceived as nonreligious or profane. Every meaningful act was seen as religious or sacred. Professor Robert Bellah of the University of California at Berkeley argues that in the West the split between the sacred and the profane or the differentiation of religion from other aspects of life did not really begin until about the time of the Protestant Reformation. He refers to that period as "early modern." Beginning with the early modern period onward to the present, religion has become more and more differentiated from Western culture. Thus, for example, it is no longer assumed that an American is a Protestant, whereas it is still largely assumed that a Thai is a Buddhist.

The question has been asked, "Can someone understand a religion in which he or she does not believe?" As the previous discussion of the nature of religion indicates, belief in the truth claims of a religious tradition is not a prerequisite for engaging in its study or even for understanding (i.e., making sense of) its beliefs and historical forms. The study of religion, however, does demand empathy and sympathy. To engage in the study of another religion for the purpose of proving that one's own is superior can only result in a distorted understanding of that tradition. Or, for that matter, if one who professes no religious belief approaches the study of religion with an inhibiting scepticism, then the beauty and richness of religion will be lost. For the believer, the study of another religious tradition should enhance his or her own faith-understanding; for the nonbeliever (i.e., agnostic), the study of religion should open up new dimensions of the human spirit.

The objective study of religion should be undertaken because of its inherent significance—because the understanding of cultures and societies, indeed, of humankind, is severely limited when such study is ignored. The study of our own tradition from its own particular creedal or denominational perspective is justifiably a part of our profession of faith. However, such study should not close us off from a sympathetic understanding of other religious traditions. Rather, such inquiry should open us to what we share in common with other religious persons, as well as to what is genuinely unique about our own religious beliefs and traditions.

Is the study of religion relevant today? The authors of this series believe the answer is a resounding "Yes!" The United States—indeed, the world—is in the midst of a profound transition period. The crisis confronting nations today cannot be reduced merely to economic inflation, political instability, and social upheaval. It is also one of values and convictions. The time has passed when we can ignore our crying need to reexamine such basic questions as who we are and where we are going—as individuals, as communities, and as a nation. The interest in Islam on the part of many American blacks, experimentation with various forms of Asian religions by the "Age of Aquarius" generation, and a resurgence of Christian piety on college campuses are particular responses to the crisis of identity through which we are currently passing.

The serious study of religion in the world today is not only legitimate but necessary. Today we need all of the forces we can muster in order to restore a sense of individual worth, moral community, and value direction. The sympathetic study of religion can contribute toward these goals and can be of assistance in helping us to recover an awareness of our common humanity too long overshadowed by our preoccupation with technological and material achievement. As has been popularly said, we have conquered outer space at the expense of inner space.

But why study non-Western religions? The reason is quite simple. We no longer live in relative isolation from the cultures of Asia and Africa. As a consequence the marketplace of ideas, values, and faiths is much broader than it used to be. We are in contact with them through popular books and the news media, but for the most part our acquaintance is superficial at best. Rather than looking at the religions imbedded in these cultures as quaint or bizarre—an unproductive enterprise—we should seek genuine understanding of them in the expectation of broadening, deepening, and hopefully clarifying our own personal identity and direction. The study of religion is, then, a twofold enterprise: engaging the religion(s) as it is, and engaging ourselves in the light of that religion.

The Argus Communications Major World Religions Series attempts to present the religious traditions of Judaism, Christianity, Islam, Hinduism, Buddhism, China, and Africa in their unity and variety. On the one hand, the authors interpret the traditions about which they are writing as a faith or a world view which instills the lives of their adherents with value, meaning, and direction. On the other hand, each volume attempts to analyze a particular religion in terms of its historical and cultural settings. This latter dimension means that the authors are interested in the present form of a religious tradition as well as its past development. How can Christianity or Judaism speak to the problems confronting Americans today? What are some of the new religions of Africa, and are they displacing traditional beliefs and world views? Can Maoism be considered the new religion of China? Is traditional Hinduism able to cope with India's social, economic, and political change? The answers to such questions form a legitimate and important part of the content of the series.

The author of each volume is a serious student and teacher of the tradition about which he or she is writing. Each has spent considerable time in countries where that religious tradition is part of the culture. Furthermore, as individuals, the authors are committed to the positive value the proper study of religion can have for students in these times of rapid social, political, and economic change. We hope that the series succeeds in its attempt to present the world's religions not as something "out there," a curiosity piece of times past, but as a subject of study relevant to the needs of our times.

Preface

This volume would not have been possible without the help of numerous friends throughout Buddhist Asia who have helped me in my study of Buddhism during the past decade. In particular the author would like to mention Eshin Nishimura and Shojun Bando of the Japanese Rinzai Zen and Pure Land traditions, respectively; Vichit Ratna Dhiravamsa, Chao Khun Rajavaramuni, Sommai Premehit, and Singkha Wannasai of the Thai Therevada tradition; and the late K. N. Jayatilleke of the University of Sri Lanka.

My wife, Nancy, has not only shared my interests in Asian cultures and religions but revised and greatly improved this volume.

Finally, I would like to thank the individual authors in the Major World Religions Series for their understanding and cooperation in seeing the series through; Dan Crowe, editor of Argus Communications, for his confidence in the Major World Religions Series; and Joan Lathen for editing the book on behalf of Argus.

Prologue

Satien was finishing his last year in the college preparatory high school course in Chiang Mai when his father died in a tragic collision while driving from northern Thailand to Bangkok, the capital. Following Thai Buddhist custom, Satien was then ordained as a novice monk for a brief period of time in order to gain merit by the performance of this religious act. Thus, it was believed, his father would be reborn into a favorable state in his next lifetime. Satien had planned to be ordained after he graduated from high school and before he started his university course in Bangkok. His father's sudden death merely hastened what had already been planned for him.

Satien had seen many ordinations before. Many of his friends in his home village had been ordained when they were much younger. They had come from poor families, and becoming novices provided them with free education in monastery schools in secular as well as religious subjects. Upon the completion of junior high school, most of them had left the Buddhist monastic life for secular jobs. Of course, a few remained for further education. And an even smaller number would dedicate their entire lifetime to the Lord Buddha as celibate, saffron-robed monks. However, the great majority of young men, like Satien, follow the custom of entering the monkhood for three months or less. Years ago becoming a monk was one of the only ways to be educated. For middle-class Thais, it still remains as a symbol of socialization into Thai society. As in Satien's case, ordination also has the religious signification of earning merit, especially for one's parents. Such merit is based in two beliefs known as the law of *karma* and *samsara,* or rebirth. These terms are from Sanskrit, an ancient Indian language and one of the languages in which many of the original Buddhist scriptures were written in India nearly two thousand years ago.

In Buddhism the law of *karma* is usually interpreted to mean that every act, both in intention and performance, has a consequence. The concept of *samsara* reflects the equally important belief that life is a continuum not limited to one physical lifetime or even by the condition of being human. Thus, Buddhists believe that existences are interconnected and continuous and that the state into which one may be reborn can be human, subhuman, or superhuman. To understand the purpose behind Satien's ordination one must understand the Buddhist teachings of *karma* and *samsara*.

From a practical standpoint, ordination into the Buddhist monkhood is a social custom. Yet unlike ordination into the ministry, priesthood, or monastic orders in Christianity, the step Satien is about to undertake is not necessarily a lifetime commitment. On the contrary, in Thailand only a small percentage of those ordained spend most of their lives as monks, or *bhikkhus* (mendicant or homeless wanderers). Ordination in this sense might be compared to a bar mitzvah or confirmation, ceremonies marking full participation in the Jewish and Christian communities. While these events are meaningful personally for the individuals involved, they are also social rites of passage that a young Jew or Christian undertakes usually between the ages of twelve and fifteen. Similarly, in traditional Buddhist countries like Thailand, Laos, Burma, and Cambodia, a young man will be ordained for a relatively brief period during which time he will receive rather intensive instruction in the rudiments of Buddhist thought and practice. In this way he is socialized into his society just as you may have been socialized into your religious community.

In sum, Satien's ordination cannot be understood by us as interested observers unless we know something about the theory of *karma* and *samsara* and also about the social context in which his ordination ceremony is taking place. We cannot understand Buddhism unless we try to learn both about its teachings or world view and its social/cultural realities.

Before his ordination at the temple, a special "spirit-calling" ceremony is held at Satien's home. This ceremony has little to do with Buddhism, coming instead from an ancient set of religious beliefs and practices usually labeled animism in the West. Animistic religion is rooted in the belief that people and/or things have an unpredictable and mysterious side or are possessed by spirits. These spirits may be responsible for ill health, for good luck on journeys, and so forth. Certainly, whenever an unusual or dangerous undertaking occurs, many Thais believe some kind of ceremony must be held to placate these spirits. Although the people of Thailand and other Southeast Asian countries revere Buddhism, their religious practice also reflects elements of animistic belief. In the case of an ordination or even a wedding—both potentially dangerous times for they signal a change in status—a ceremony may be held to "call the spirit(s)" of the person(s) involved in order that the spirit(s) will not be angered or ignored.

xvi

In Satien's case the spirit-calling ceremony acts, in effect, as the first stage of his ordination. Physically he is prepared for the ordination: his facial hair is shaved off and he is dressed in white indicating that he, like the Buddha before him, is giving up worldly pursuits. Seated on the floor of his home with his hands placed together as a sign of respect, Satien is surrounded by the saffron robes he will wear and gift offerings from his mother and relatives to be given to the monks at the temple. The spirit-calling ceremony is not conducted by a Buddhist monk but by a specially trained layman sometimes called a spirit doctor or teacher. These teachers have a tradition distinct from Buddhism, although it has been influenced by Buddhist teachings. They have learned what to chant from manuals and have been taught how to chant or preach in a particular manner aimed at enticing the spirits of the subjects away from previous attachments. Thus, the spirit-calling ceremony is a way of getting a person all together before beginning a new venture or changing his status.

From Satien's ordination, then, something else can be learned about Buddhism—namely, that Buddhism is a complex cultural reality with non-Buddhist elements incorporated into it. The Buddhist teachings of *karma* and *samsara* do not help to explain the spirit calling preliminary to Satien's ordination. Indeed, even the social significance of the ordination as a ceremony observing the passage of a young male into adult membership in Thai society sheds only some light on the meaning of the spirit-calling event. Its interpretation demands some knowledge of non-Buddhist traditions and the way they have been transformed within Thai Buddhism. Buddhism does not differ radically from Christianity or Judaism on this point, however. Think for a moment how Judaism and Christianity adapted ancient agricultural celebrations to Passover and Easter. Every religion has incorporated within itself cultural elements not originally part of that tradition.

Later that evening Satien goes to the monastery (called *wat* in Thai) where he will be ordained the next day. He meets once more with the monk who has been instructing him in the vows he will take during the ceremony and in the duties and customs to be observed during his tenure as a novice monk. While a man over twenty who is ordained to full monkhood pledges to observe 227 rules of discipline, Satien as a novice is expected to follow only the following 10: abstention from taking life, stealing, sexual unchastity, lying, intoxicants or drugs, eating after noon, participating in entertainments, costuming or perfuming the body, sleeping on a comfortable bed, and receiving money. Central to the novitiate ordination is the pledge of obedience to these vows.

The ceremony begins with Satien being carried around the temple on the shoulders of an uncle in a procession consisting of family and friends. Sometimes the person being ordained is dressed in princely clothing and rides a horse after the example of the Lord Buddha, who renounced his royal position to become a mendicant. Satien then enters the hall where he presents his robes to the abbot, or monastery superior. He kneels, bowing with forehead to the floor, and requests permission to enter the monastic order (or *sangha,* meaning "group," "fellowship," or "community") so that he may work for the destruction of worldly sorrow and the attainment of perfect freedom, or Nirvana. The abbot then returns the robes to Satien and reminds him of the perishable nature of the body and of the changeable nature of all things in this world. With the help of other monks Satien dresses in his new set of saffron robes. He then returns to be presented to the abbot by his teacher. After pledging obedience to the Buddha, his teaching (known as *dharma,* or truth), and his community (the *sangha*), and after taking his vows, the ceremony ends. Satien now becomes a member of the Buddhist monastic order, the most important religious institution in Asian Buddhist countries. There he will receive basic instruction in the teachings of the Buddha and the practices of his institution. In this way Satien becomes a part of a religious culture which began in India over twenty-five hundred years ago and which has had a continuous history in a variety of forms throughout most of Asia.

By looking at an ordination ceremony, a wide variety of questions are raised about Buddhism—its history, culture, social context, and teachings. This volume touches upon all of these aspects of the Buddhist tradition and reveals that Buddhism is much more than simply a teaching about an ultimate goal, called Nirvana, or a church in Thailand, Sri Lanka, or Japan. It is both of these and everything in between as well.

Four white-robed boys prepare for ordination.
In the background is the funeral carriage
for a Buddhist abbot.

Part I
The Birth and Growth of Buddhism

Why study Buddhism? What does a study of an esoteric, oriental religion have to do with me? Not so long ago these would have been valid questions. Only a handful of scholars and a few world travelers bothered to delve into what were considered to be oriental mysteries and esoteric practices. Now, however, the world has changed. The media brings Katmandu and Kyoto, Bangkok and Bali into our living rooms nearly every day, and it may no longer seem exceptional when someone we know practices Zen meditation.

As the world shrinks and we Westerners begin to rub shoulders more frequently with Buddhists, Hindus, and Muslims, we need to understand the world as they understand it. We cannot embark on such a journey of understanding without some background, however. The fact that the West has a rich religious heritage—primarily Jewish/Christian—will help guide you through unfamiliar ground. On this particular journey you will need to use your imagination as well as your mind in order to try to experience Buddhism as the living faith of millions of people. You will visit temples, see festivals, listen to traditional stories, try your hand at meditation, and study the teachings of the Buddha. If you can become thoroughly involved in the varied aspects of the Buddhist tradition, you can begin to see Buddhism from the inside and not merely as a curious spectator. Try to see this volume as a guidebook to what Buddhists believe and how they express their beliefs in practice. The journey will not always be easy. You might stumble over unfamiliar words and ideas, and the geography will sometimes be strange. Yet, the effort promises to be challenging and worthwhile.

Do you know which of the great world religions has had the widest geographic and cultural development and popularity? You are right if you guessed Buddhism. From its original homeland in northern India, Buddhism spread to southern India and Ceylon (now Sri Lanka) and then continued east to Southeast Asia where it became the state religion of Burma, Thailand, and much of Indochina. Another form of Buddhism traveled east from northern India into China, Korea, and

1

Japan and later into Tibet where it flourished until the Chinese occupation in 1951. Buddhist communities are also found in the United States and Europe. Not only has Buddhism spread over a large area, but it has been around for a long time—over twenty-five hundred years. Because of its wide area of influence, it naturally developed different teachings and practices. For these reasons, the theme of Part I will be the unity and diversity within the Buddhist religious tradition.

Part I begins by acquainting you with the story of the Buddha's life and the founding of the Buddhist religion. Then it proceeds to describe how the tradition was formed in India and how it developed in Southeast and East Asia. One of the most fascinating issues in this part is the relationship between Buddhism and secular powers. You will discover that Buddhism, as one of the most adaptable expressions of Indian thought and culture, has had a significant role to play as a political and social integrater in many Asian countries. How curious that this religion, so often characterized as being otherworldly, should have been used to legitimate political power by rulers as far ranging as Asoka in India (third century B.C.) to Wu Ti in China (sixth century A.D.) and Prince Shotoku in Japan (sixth century A.D.). While the United States has insisted on the separation of church and state throughout its history, a close relationship between religion and political power has characterized the history of both medieval Europe and Buddhist Asia.

THE BUDDHA AND THE FOUNDING OF BUDDHISM

The world's great historic religions (Judaism, Christianity, Islam, Hinduism, and Buddhism) emerged in times much like the present— times of transition and change. The sixth century B.C. gave birth not only to the Buddha but also to the prophets of Israel and to Confucius and Lao Tzu in China. All of these cultures were in the midst of gradual yet profound change giving rise to new beliefs and values. Men of insight captured the spirit of their times in visionary teachings compelling the imagination and attracting dedicated followers. In this way new religions and philosophies of life come into being.

In northern India, in what is now southern Nepal, in a place known as Lumpini, the wife of the chief of the Sakya clan gave birth to a son named Siddhartha, meaning "one who accomplishes his aim." This child was destined to become a Buddha (a fully enlightened one) whose teachings were to grow into one of the world's most revered religions.

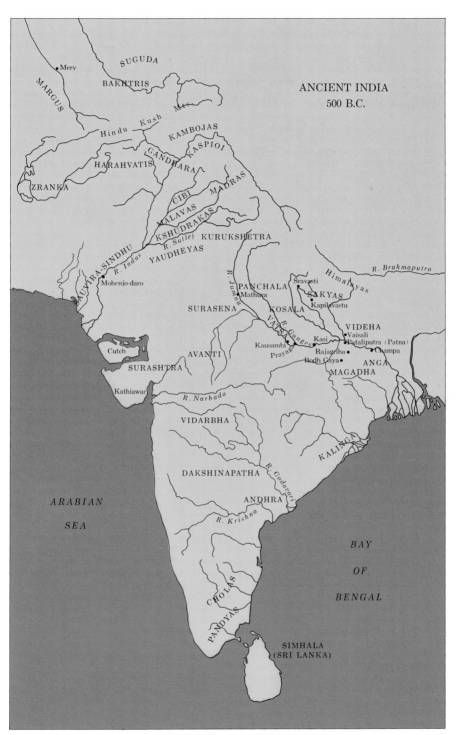

ANCIENT INDIA
500 B.C.

Merv

SUGUDA

BAKHTRIS

MARGUS

Hindu Kush

KAMBOJAS

KASPIOI

GANDHARA

HARAHVATIS

ZRANKA

CIBI

MADRAS

MALAVAS

KSHUDRAKAS

KURUKSHETRA

R. Sutlej

AUVIRA-SINDHU

R. Indus

YAUDHEYAS

Mohenjo-daro

R. Brahmaputra

R. Jumna

PANCHALA

Sravesti

Himalayas

Mathura

SAKYAS

SURASENA

KOSALA

Kapilavastu

VATSA

R. Ganges

VIDEHA

Vaisali

Kasi

Pataliputra (Patna)

Kausambi

Prayaga

Rajagriha

Champa

Cutch

AVANTI

Bodh Gaya

ANGA

SURASHTRA

MAGADHA

Kathiawar

R. Narbada

VIDARBHA

KALINGA

DAKSHINAPATHA

R. Godavari

ANDHRA

ARABIAN

R. Krishna

SEA

BAY

OF

BENGAL

CHOLAS

PANDYAS

SIMHALA
(SRI LANKA)

3

At the time of the future Buddha's birth (563 B.C.), this part of northern India was undergoing far-reaching changes. Politically, small clan groups like the Sakyas were being absorbed into larger kingdoms such as Magadha and Kosala. Economically, this period was marked by the increasing development of towns, a money economy, and a nonagricultural leisure class. Religiously, teachers were emerging and, like the Buddha, were speaking to the felt needs of people whose way of life was in the process of change. In the sixth century B.C., the traditional priestly, sacrificial religion of northern India known as Brahmanism was being challenged, especially in the area on the eastern edge of the center of Brahmanic power—an area where such teachers as the Buddha and Makhali Gosala, the founder of the Indian religious sect called Jainism, taught. Furthermore, the more primitive, animistic beliefs of the rural, agricultural population were not satisfied by Brahmanic religion, a religion of the better educated and more sophisticated town folk.

Briefly, these were the historical conditions out of which Buddhism grew. While distant in time, those transitional years were similar to the present age—an age of uncertainty and change, of the search for the meaning of life. While our own Western civilization differs markedly from that of northern India in the sixth century B.C., it shares something of the confusion and challenge which are part of all transitional periods, when old institutions and ways of life are giving way to new forms, and old philosophies are encountering new teachings. Indeed, it may even be the case that the sixth century B.C. characterizes the present as well as or better than any other historical period.

The Buddha emerged in this great transitional period. He was one of several major religious teachers who followed a wandering type of life going from place to place and attracting small but dedicated followings. The primary religion of his time, Brahmanism, focused on the performance of sacrificial rituals in honor of a wide variety of gods. These rituals aimed to secure the gods' favor so they might act on behalf of the sacrificers. The sacred rituals of this sacrificial religion were conducted by a priestly class, or caste, known as Brahmans. In the sixth century B.C., this priestly, sacrificial religion was being challenged by several nomadic religious cults. Wandering teachers of the type represented by the Buddha formed small groups of religious seekers who followed an informal code of religious discipline and affirmed their loyalty to the teaching of their master. Perhaps the closest examples of such religious groups in Western culture are the mendicant

4

religious orders such as the Roman Catholic Franciscans which were so important in medieval Europe.

The biographical accounts of the Buddha are filled with myth and legend. This does not mean that these accounts are false or that the Buddha was not a historical person, but rather, that the stories of Buddha in the sacred scriptures of Buddhism were written primarily to evoke faith and trust in his power and his teaching. In this regard, the Buddhist scriptures do not differ from the scriptures of any religious tradition. The story of the life of the Buddha, therefore, does not merely narrate episodes about an exceptional man. It sets forth a pattern or outline for a new way of understanding and living in the world, just as the life of Jesus in the Christian Gospels provides a model of humility and love. Above all, the accounts of the life of the Buddha tell the story of a man who discovered the truth and proclaimed that all people who follow the path he charted would find the same final and liberating goal.

There are varying accounts of the Buddha's biography from different sectors of the Buddhist world. The story presented here is taken primarily from the tradition known as the Theravada (Teachings of the Elders), whose sacred scriptures and commentaries are written in Pali, an ancient religious language of India.

The Buddha was born into an aristocratic or ruling class family. He was a prince, the son of the ruler of the Sakya clan, which was soon to be incorporated into the larger kingdom of Magadha. The birth of the Buddha was announced by four angels who received the baby in a golden net and declared, "Rejoice, O queen! A mighty son has been born to you." Similar signs accompanied the birth of Jesus. But while the setting of Jesus' kingship is a carpenter's family and the stable of an inn in Bethlehem, the Buddha's royal nature is declared wholeheartedly:

> Then the Brahma angels, after receiving him on their golden net, delivered him to the four guardian angels, who received him from their hands on a rug which was made of the skins of black antelopes, and was soft to the touch, being such as is used on state occasions; and the guardian angels delivered him to men who received him on a coil of fine cloth; and the men let him out of their hands on the ground, where he stood and faced the east. There, before him, lay many thousands of worlds, like a great open court; and in them, gods and men, making offerings to him of perfumes, garlands, and so on, were saying, "Great Being! There is none your equal, much less your superior."[1]

The theme of Siddhartha's royal status is repeated throughout the story of the Buddha's youth to emphasize the magnitude of his decision to give up the luxury of his station and follow a religious path. One of the earliest episodes in the biography of the Buddha illustrating this tension between religious and secular goals occurred at his name-giving ceremony. At that time, eight learned fortune-tellers predicted that Siddhartha would become either a universal monarch or a Buddha. Siddhartha's father, distressed at the thought that his son might follow a religious path rather than becoming a great king, said, "It will never do for my son to become a Buddha. What I would wish to see is my son exercising sovereign rule and authority over the four great continents and the two thousand adjoining islands. . . ."[2] Acting on this wish the king surrounded his son with everything his heart could desire. When Siddhartha was sixteen, his father built three palaces for him, one for each season (hot, cool, monsoon) where he was attended by dancing girls and musicians. That same year he married and in due course had a son. During the next seventeen years the Buddhist texts tell us that Siddhartha was "wholly given over to pleasure." Yet the time was soon to come when he would choose another way.

One of the best-known stories in Buddhism is the episode describing Siddhartha's decision to renounce a life of luxury. According to this legend, the Buddha was out riding in his pleasure gardens when he chanced upon four types of people he had never seen before: an old man, a diseased man, a dead man, and a mendicant monk. The sight of each person greatly distressed him. When he returned to the palace, ". . . that magnificent apartment, as splendid as the palace of the chief of the gods, began to seem like a cemetery filled with dead bodies . . . ; and the three modes of existence [past, present, future] appeared like houses on fire. After sighing, 'How oppressive and stifling it is!', his mind turned ardently to retiring from the world."[3] And so Siddhartha embarked on a mendicant path for six years, studying with teachers of Yoga and other philosophies. At one point he nearly died from the

A statue of the Buddha practicing austerities before his enlightenment.

severity of his ascetic practices. He came to believe that such austerities would not lead to enlightenment and that a religious way which sought genuine understanding and knowledge would have to be a middle way between the extremes of worldliness and asceticism. For this reason Buddhism is often called the religion of the Middle Way.

After the six years of experimentation with different teachings and disciplines, Siddhartha's effort finally ended in victory. The texts describe his enlightenment in vivid detail, especially the last onslaught of Mara, the Buddhist equivalent of Satan. This final temptation occurred just prior to Siddhartha's attainment of Buddhahood, or the full realization of his spiritual goal and vocation. The temptation functioned as a final test of Siddhartha's worthiness for a higher calling and, in this regard, is not unlike Jesus' temptation recounted in the Gospel of Matthew. There Satan tried to entice Jesus from his religious vocation with promises of worldly power and satisfactions. Just as Jesus' temptation occurred immediately before he began his teaching ministry, so Mara's test of Siddhartha occurred just prior to the full realization of his religious vocation as the Buddha—the Enlightened One, or Sakyamuni, the "sage of the Sakyas."

With his goal realized, the Buddha spent the next forty-five years teaching the truths he had discovered about the nature of life. These teachings are summarized in an oft-repeated formula which appears as part of the Buddha's first public teaching (see Part II). The formula is called the Four Noble Truths: (1) there is a fundamental dissatisfaction or unease about life, (2) this dissatisfaction is rooted in the human tendency toward grasping and selfish attachments, (3) this dissatisfaction can be eliminated if this grasping nature can be corrected, (4) the way to correct selfish craving is charted out in the Eightfold Path which includes moral virtue, contemplative practices, and the attainment of wisdom. These doctrines form a small portion of an extensive Buddhist literature in which the Buddha appears fundamentally as a teacher. Dialogues between the Buddha and his disciples, other religious seekers, and lay persons show the central importance of the teaching function of the early Buddhist community.

HOW THE EARLY BUDDHIST COMMUNITY GREW IN INDIA

The development of Buddhism in India in the sixth century B.C. was not unlike that of other religious traditions. It began as a sect, a small group of followers around a leader with a distinctive teaching. Some sects remain small, having little impact on the culture in which they are found. Others, however, gain in popularity and size. Such was the case with Buddhism. By the third century B.C., less than three hundred years after the death of its founder, Buddhism became one of the most important religions in India. Popularity has its price, however. In the development of religions, popularity and increase in size inevitably necessitate changes and accommodations of both doctrinal and institutional forms and practices. Such changes occurred in Buddhism. On the one hand, they resulted in the proliferation of different Buddhist schools; on the other, Buddhism made so many accommodations that it was simply absorbed into Hinduism which had become the dominant religion of India. What was the nature of the community of followers that developed around the Buddha? What distinctive directions did Buddhism take in its early history?

Early Indian Buddhism was primarily a monastic religion. The Buddha withdrew from the life of a householder in order to devote himself fully to a spiritual quest. In this pursuit he was not unique. At the time there were other religious mendicant teachers who were apparently supported in their quest by lay persons and who attracted greater or lesser numbers of followers depending, we would assume, on the appeal of their teachings. These groups resided on the outskirts of towns and villages where they were protected from the hustle and bustle of everyday life, yet were close enough to secure food and other necessities. The Buddhist texts relate the story of the Buddha's ministry in considerable detail, and one is struck by the variety of persons who became his followers although the Buddha's message appealed primarily to the educated classes. The Buddha is pictured as a teacher rather than as a yogic ascetic who performs miraculous feats as a result of his extraordinary training. The middle way of Buddhism and the role of the Buddha as a teacher meant that the Buddha had rejected the yogic model in favor of the teaching one.

The early Buddhist community (known as *sangha,* or assemblage of monk-followers) withdrew from the mundane world of commerce and family responsibilities so that its members could devote themselves full time to spiritual reflection and practice. The organization of that community during the Buddha's lifetime must have been very simple. It is easy to imagine that as the Buddha's followers became more numerous they began to split off either singly or in small groups. Yet the ideal remained one of simplicity and detachment symbolized by the famous injunction in one of the texts—"let the monk wander alone like a rhinoceros"—or in the words of the *Dhammapada,* one of the most important Buddhist texts: "He who controls his hand, he who controls his feet, he who controls his speech, he who is well controlled, he who delights inwardly, who is collected, who is solitary and content, him they call a monk."

In actual practice, then, the monastic community provided an environment protected from the demands of the world where one could pursue a religious path single-mindedly. In Buddhism an important part of this path is the practice of meditation. Because a meditative way of life is extremely difficult to follow when one has incessant demands of family obligations and job, a monastic life offers an appropriate environment for meditation, reflection, and study. In one of the best-known meditation texts in the Theravada Buddhist tradition, the Buddha advises: "A monk who wishes to practice mindfulness should go to the forest, to the foot of a tree or some empty place, sit down with his legs crossed, keep his body straight and his mind alert." How difficult this would be in a noisy, bustling household with all its distractions!

The early Buddhist community was distinctive and unique in comparison to the way most people lived. It had to be in order for the followers of the Buddha to devote themselves wholeheartedly to the pursuit of the highest spiritual goal, which the Buddhist community called Nirvana. Consequently, both as a symbol of a very different life-style and, practically, to afford a context for contemplation and reflection, the basic institution of early Buddhism as a monastic religion was not cut off from the world. As mendicants, Buddhist monks were dependent upon the laity for their physical and material well-being. For this reason, the monk was called a *bhikkhu,* one who depends on others for food and other necessities. They were, then, in constant contact with lay people. Furthermore, the Buddha and his community had as one of their major goals the propagation of the *dharma,* or teaching. Many of the Buddhist texts relate episodes where the Buddha is discussing questions of religious truth with lay people, and in some texts the Buddha speaks with great admiration of the wisdom of lay persons.

In sum, the Buddhist monastic order was an important symbol of a community devoted to the pursuit of spiritual truth. It provided a context in which a path to that truth could be followed, and it functioned as the medium through which the Buddha and his followers taught. Later some Buddhist monastic communities became the most important educational centers in India just as did certain religious institutions in medieval Europe.

How did Buddhism develop as a monastic institution? This question is difficult to answer. In general, however, the tendency was to move from an individual mendicant pattern to more complex and communal forms. This communal pattern developed from the custom adopted by the mendicant religious groups of seeking shelter near towns during the monsoon or rainy season. Gradually, the period of time lengthened until finally it became common practice for Buddhist monks to live in settled communities all year rather than following a wandering pattern. This latter practice is still found in Buddhist countries; however, today monks who "wander lonely as a rhinoceros" are very much the exception rather than the rule.

A similar tendency toward complexity characterizes other aspects of institutional Buddhism in India. The ordination procedure for admission of monks into the order, the rules of discipline, and the *dharma,* or collections of teachings, became increasingly more elaborate as the institution grew. Whereas in the early days the Buddha admitted people into his order with no specific ceremony, a more elaborate ritual gradually developed which demanded the presence of a set number of fully ordained monks and a clearly defined procedure. The rules of the order increased to over two hundred, and a bimonthly ceremony on the days of the full and half moon was held to rehearse them and confess any infraction against them. As the oral collections of Buddhist teaching grew, their narrative form changed to a more systematic and philosophical nature.

All of these developments did not take place simply by historical accident and happenstance. Rather, the growth of the order, the development of the rules of discipline (*vinaya*), and the systematic formation of Buddhist teachings into a canon[4] took place through a series of meetings, or councils. According to Buddhist historical accounts, councils took place immediately after the death of the Buddha and then at one-hundred-year intervals during the next three hundred years. Other general meetings for the purpose of codifying teachings and elaborating rules of behavior have been held throughout the history of Buddhism in all Buddhist countries. The most recent council was held in Rangoon from 1954 to 1956 upon the occasion of the 2500th anniversary of the Buddha's death. Buddhists from all over Asia attended, and a new edition of the canon of Theravada Buddhism was begun.

The first three Buddhist councils established the basic doctrines and rules of monastic discipline. These meetings also formalized the sectarian beginnings of the two major divisions of Buddhism—the Theravada (Teachings of the Elders) and the Mahayana (Great Vehicle). The first so-called council was held shortly after the Buddha's

11

death. The site was Rajagriha, a place where the Buddha must have taught and where a large number of his followers must have been concentrated. This meeting was probably little more than an oral recitation of the rules of monastic behavior and the teachings of the Buddha which had developed up to that point. This recital established the general outline of two sections of Buddhist canonical writings— the *vinaya,* or rules of monastic discipline, and the *sutra* teachings, many of which occur in dialogue form. However, as was true in Christianity and Judaism, the authoritative teachings of Buddhism continued to increase and develop.

While the first council was probably no more than a review and simple codification of rules and teachings, the second, held at Vaisali a century later, marks the formal beginning of schism in Indian Buddhism. This schism grew up around disagreement about the disciplinary rules and anticipated the formation of two distinct traditions we now call the Theravada, which considers itself to be the tradition closest to the teachings and practices of the earliest Buddhist community, and the Mahayana, which at the time of the second council was called the Great Assembly (Mahasanghika), indicating the large number of monks who agreed with its teachings. According to the Theravada historical tradition, the disagreement between the two schools centered around various rules of behavior. Examination of some of these rules clarifies the position taken by the Theravada tradition: monks cannot take food after midday; they must attend the recitation of the monastic rules in the same monastic center; they cannot drink toddy (a mild intoxicant made from sugar palm); they cannot use a rug with a fringe; and they cannot accept gold and silver. According to the Buddhist chronicles of Sri Lanka,[5] the council decided in favor of a strict enforcement of these rules. However, a large group of monks led by a faction from an area called Vajji disagreed with the ruling elders and broke away. Thus as early as one hundred years after the Buddha's death we find an anticipation of the division of Buddhism into the more liberal "great tradition" (Mahayana) and the more traditional or conservative Theravada. Later differences included significant reinterpretations of doctrine as well as disciplinary rules.

The most famous of the early councils was the third, reputed to have been called by Asoka (third century B.C.), one of the most powerful rulers in the entire history of India. The chronicles record that Asoka was converted to Buddhism shortly after a series of battles which had produced one of the most extensive unified Indian kingdoms prior to the modern period. Appalled at the amount of blood spilled in these campaigns, Asoka became a follower of the Buddha, upholding a doctrine of nonviolence. While the legend that he became a monk for a brief period is dubious, archaeological evidence supports the picture of Asoka as a benevolent and humanitarian ruler dedicated to the material and spiritual welfare of his people.

With the growing popularity of Buddhism, the material prosperity of the monastic order greatly increased. More and more people entered the order for their own material benefit to the detriment of the practice and teaching of Buddhism. As a result, Asoka called a third council to codify the teachings of the Buddha. According to the historical chronicles of Sri Lanka, this council concluded that the most orthodox teaching was the Vibhajjavada (the "teaching of analytical reasoning"), maintained by the Theravada sect of Buddhism. In addition to setting forth a particular teaching or doctrine, this council also may have dispatched missionaries from India to several areas including Sri Lanka, peninsular Southeast Asia, and even the Mediterranean area.

Asoka's religious faith expressed itself in a variety of ways. He toured the sacred sites of Buddhism, erecting commemorative pillars at the places where the Buddha was born, enlightened, and so on. The teachings recorded on these stone pillars emphasize the virtues of righteousness, compassion, liberality, truthfulness, purity, gentleness, and tolerance. In practical terms Asoka advocated nonviolence to living things, obedience to parents and elders, reverence to teachers, liberality toward friends, and religious tolerance. His religion obviously stressed individual development and social virtues rather than rites and ceremonies.

He emphasized the performance of good deeds and the accumulation of merit in order to be reborn in one of the Buddhist heavens. Merit and the reward of a heavenly rebirth are among the most important teachings of popular Buddhism, and they probably came into vogue during the reign of King Asoka.

During the three hundred years from the death of the Buddha to the reign of King Asoka, then, Buddhism had developed in surprising ways. It had changed from a relatively small sectarian group of mendicant wanderers to a popular religion espoused by one of India's greatest monarchs. Popular piety took the shape of pilgrimage to the major sites associated with the life of the Buddha and his community. Reliquary mounds called *cetiyas,* reputed to contain relics of the Buddha's body or possessions, were erected at these sites. Devotees undoubtedly believed that circumambulating (i.e., walking around) these mounds not only honored the founder of the Buddhist religion but also had some special magical power. Similarly, medieval Chris-

tians believed that the relics of Jesus and the saints of the early church held magical power and considered the sites where the relics were kept as holy.

On a more sophisticated level, the teachings of the Buddha became more elaborate. They came to be codified in different canons. New sectarian differences arose. The earliest scriptures depict the Buddha as a teacher rather than as some sort of superhuman being. His main mission in life was to teach the way to overcome suffering. Given the importance of the Buddha's teaching (*dharma*), it is not surprising to find that Buddhist monasteries later became the most important educational centers in India. Indeed, in the eighth and ninth centuries A.D., when Buddhism had long since been overshadowed by Hinduism in most parts of India, Nalanda University and other Buddhist universities continued as centers of higher learning.

Buddhism thrived in many parts of India in the early centuries A.D. Records of Chinese Buddhist pilgrims who came to India during the fifth and sixth centuries testify to the flourishing conditions of Buddhism in Gandhara in the west, Mathura near New Delhi, and Magadha farther to the east in the Ganges river valley. Moreover, archaeological evidence from this period shows highly developed forms of Buddhist art and architecture at Sarnath outside of present-day Benares and the famous Buddhist caves of Ajanta and Bagh near Bombay. After the middle of the seventh century, however, the fortunes of Buddhism in India began to decline. In some parts of the country, for relatively brief periods of time, the light of Buddhism would blaze forth again as in the tenth and eleventh centuries in the north under the patronage of the Pala dynasty. Yet, with these exceptions and in spite of the continued florescence of Buddhist education at Nalanda, Vikramasila, and Odantapuri, the creative spirit of Buddhism burned brighter in other parts of Asia.

A pillar of King Asoka, with three lions
supporting the Wheel of the Law.

BUDDHISM IN SOUTHEAST ASIA

The predominant form of Buddhism in Southeast Asia is the Theravada, known for its orthodoxy, purity of life and conduct, and monastic organization. Historically, this tradition grew out of the sect of Indian Buddhism known as the Vibhajjavada, but Theravada Buddhism as it is known today developed primarily in Sri Lanka (formerly called Ceylon).

Sri Lanka

Buddhism was introduced to Sri Lanka by Mahinda, the son of King Asoka, and his sister, Sanghamitta, in the middle of the third century B.C. and flourished there without interruption until the fifth century A.D. Extensive monastic ruins in the ancient capital of Anuradhapura give ample evidence of the magnificence of this period. The Chinese traveler Fa-hsien, who visited Sri Lanka in the early fifth century A.D., writes that sixty thousand monks lived in hundreds of monasteries throughout the land and that the king always prepared sufficient food to feed about five thousand monks at any time! Early in this period (first century A.D.) the canon of Theravada Buddhism much as it is known today was written in Pali, and in the sixth century the most famous commentaries on many of these texts were written in Sri Lanka by Buddhaghosa, a monk. These commentaries are still standard works for Buddhist scholars in Theravada countries even though additional treatises continue to be written.

Buddhism suffered a decline in Sri Lanka from the sixth to the eleventh centuries but experienced a renaissance between the twelfth and fourteenth centuries. By this time Buddhism was no longer practiced in India, having been ultimately destroyed by Muslim conquest in the eleventh century. Therefore, it is quite natural to find that the dominant Buddhist influence in Southeast Asia came not from mainland India but from Sri Lanka, its sister island to the south, during one of its exceptionally powerful periods.

Buddhism in Sri Lanka suffered renewed declines between the fourteenth and nineteenth centuries, however, when Tamil incursions were followed by Portuguese, Dutch, and finally British invasions. The Portuguese, who dominated the island from about 1540 to 1660, destroyed monasteries and libraries and pillaged temple treasures. Neither the Dutch nor the British persecuted Buddhists as the Portuguese had done, but through policies of indifference and favoritism to Christians, the practice of Buddhism continued to deteriorate until the latter part of the nineteenth century when a Buddhist revival helped spark a new sense of national pride. This fledgling nationalistic movement grew in strength, and Sri Lanka eventually won its independence in 1956. Today Buddhism in Sri Lanka stands as the dominant religion on the island and an important element of that country's cultural and political traditions.

Burma

The early history of Buddhism in Burma points to two quite distinct traditions. The earliest Buddhist presence is Theravada. It dates from at least the fifth century A.D., and may even have been established by missionaries sent by King Asoka. One of the Chinese Buddhist pilgrims, I-tsing, wrote of a flourishing Theravada community in southern Burma in the area of Pegu. The northern part of the country, however, had been influenced by a different Buddhist tradition. There, Mahayana and Tantric forms of Buddhism like those which became popular in the seventh and eighth centuries in northern India and Central Asia came to dominate. According to Burmese chronicles, this type of Buddhism did not follow the teachings of the Theravada but instead practiced magic and even followed the custom of sending virgins to priests before marriage. Numerous Buddhist deities, both male and female, were also worshipped. This kind of magical Buddhism, where Buddhas were worshipped as gods, developed among the common people and, in northern India, became so indistinguishable from popular forms of Hinduism that it eventually died out as a distinct religion.

During the eleventh century, however, the Theravada form of Buddhism became dominant in most of Burma, remaining so to the present day. Anawrahta, a powerful ruler in northern Burma, extended his sway over the south, was converted to Theravada, and united the country under his rule and also under the ideology of Theravada Buddhism. The extensive remains of Buddhist monasteries and temples at Pagan in Burma provide impressive evidence of the reciprocal relationship between Buddhism and the state.

During the British colonial period, Buddhist institutions in Burma were disrupted. Christian schools and churches were opened and Buddhism was disestablished as the state religion. Discipline of the monks became more lax and morale suffered. Nevertheless, a surge of nationalism in the early twentieth century was closely tied to Buddhism, and monks lent their support and leadership to the cause of nationalism. U Nu, the prime minister of Burma from 1948 to 1962, was especially devout and labored to have Buddhism reestablished as

17

the state religion in Burma. He was deposed by his former colleague, Ne Win, partially on the grounds that Burma should be a secular state supporting the freedom of religious expression. Most Burmese still uphold Theravada Buddhism, however.

Thailand

Theravada Buddhism in Thailand, unlike that in Sri Lanka and Burma, has never been disrupted by colonial rule. Archaeological evidence points to the probability of Buddhist communities in lower and central Thailand in the early centuries A.D. The Thais who migrated into Thailand from southern China in the twelfth and thirteenth centuries also may have brought Buddhism with them. However, from the Thai chronicles it is clear that they adopted Theravada forms of Buddhism practiced by indigenous populations and later accepted Buddhist teachings and practices from Burma and Sri Lanka.

The history of Buddhism in Thailand, as in Burma, indicates distinctive northern and southern traditions. Indeed, Thailand as it is known today was not unified until the late eighteenth century after the Thais destroyed Burmese control over the north. From the nineteenth century to the present, the Thai monastic order (*sangha*) has been unified under one head; and even though there are two Theravada sects, the differences between them are minor. Monastic education throughout the country is basically the same, and religious examinations are standardized. The unity of the Thai monastic community makes it unique among Theravada Buddhist countries, and throughout its history there has been a close relationship between the order and the monarchy. The place of the *sangha* in the nation and its close relationship to the royal family are just now beginning to be questioned in the light of recent political, economic, and social upheavals.

Java and Cambodia

Non-Theravada forms of Buddhism have played relatively minor roles in Sri Lanka, Burma, and Thailand, although their presence cannot be denied. However, in Java and Cambodia, which in times past exercised considerable influence over large parts of Southeast Asia, Mahayana Buddhism dominated. Remains of elaborate shrines and temples exist as testimony to the patronage offered Mahayana and Tantric forms of Buddhism by powerful rulers in these countries.

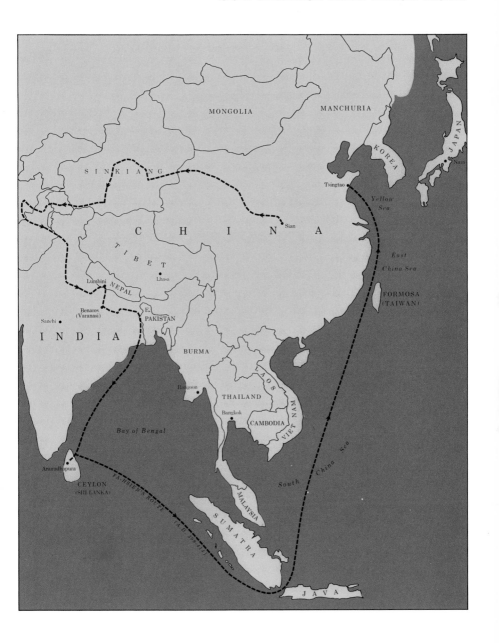

For example, Borobudur, located near Jogjakarta on Java, is one of the great religious monuments of the world. This shrine provides an idea of the splendor of the Sailendras who ruled over much of Java, Malaysia, and the southern peninsula of Thailand in the tenth and eleventh centuries. Borobudur is a *cetiya* in the form of a multileveled mountain. Its levels are covered with carvings of episodes from the Buddha's life and representations of Buddhist heavens. A journey to the top of the *cetiya* symbolizes a journey through the Buddhist heavens to the ultimate state of bliss. Correspondingly, it is a journey from lower to higher states of consciousness toward the realization of Nirvana, the highest goal of Buddhism.

Even more impressive than Borobudur is Angkor Wat, the center of an impressive temple complex built in the old Khmer capital of Cambodia, which flourished in the twelfth and thirteenth centuries. The kings of Angkor conceived themselves to be both incarnations of Hindu gods as well as future Buddhas, or *bodhisattvas* (*bodhi*—"wisdom," *sattva*—"being"). Angkor symbolizes this divinity.

Cambodia became a Theravada Buddhist country in the fourteenth century, following the Sinhalese tradition adopted by Burma, Thailand, and Laos. Only Vietnam remained to follow the Mahayana tradition, indicating the close relationship that has existed between China and Vietnam. There the Chinese sect known as Ch'an (or Zen) predominates. In Java, on the other hand, Buddhism has all but disappeared.

In summary, the popularity of Buddhism in Sri Lanka, Burma, Thailand, and Cambodia depended upon royal favor, just as it did in India. When Buddhism was espoused by kings and ruling classes, the masses soon followed suit. In this way Buddhism became a cohesive social force, a common set of beliefs, an acknowledged way of understanding the world, and an agreed-upon system of moral and ethical practices. Furthermore, in some cases, such as in ancient Cambodia, the power of a ruler was enhanced by the claim that he was a future Buddha. Such a use of Buddhism as a force for social and political integration is not unique to Southeast Asia. In Tibet, for example, the head of the state was also the head of the official state religion until the Chinese Communist takeover in 1958.

Religion cannot be properly understood apart from history, and history teaches that in traditional societies such as medieval Europe and precolonial Asia political institutions looked for religious approval to justify and solidify their own power. Such a use of religion does not mean that a given monarch cynically exploited religion for political purposes, although in some instances that might have happened. More generally it is simply the case that monarchs throughout Buddhist Asia used institutional Buddhism as a means to legitimate their power and authority. The following examination of Buddhism in East Asia will emphasize this point.

BUDDHISM IN EAST ASIA

The major schools and sects of Buddhism in China, Korea, and Japan followed the teachings of the Mahayana rather than the Theravada. As the name implies, Mahayana teachings tend to include a wide variety of doctrines, some of which vary greatly from the orthodoxy of the Theravada. For example, the Buddha, rather than being conceived of as a teacher of the truth (*dharma*), is made into both a supreme god and a number of savior gods. Also, in some forms of the Mahayana usually referred to as Tantra or Vajrayana, gods and goddesses generate the world and the highest form of self-realization is through the union of male and female forces. This inclusion of the female in the cosmic scheme of things, as well as an essential component of the path to the highest goal, is essentially foreign to the Theravada tradition (see Part II for a fuller elaboration of Mahayana teachings).

Mahayana teachings began to develop in India as early as one to two hundred years after the death of the Buddha. Early Mahayana scriptures began to appear by the first century A.D. and one of the most important Mahayana philosophers, Nagarjuna, dates from the second century. In general, however, the Mahayana and Tantric forms of Buddhism developed most extensively in East Asia. For East Asian Buddhism, China proved to be the formative cultural crucible, mediating Buddhism even farther east to Korea and Japan. For this reason, this discussion of East Asian Buddhism will focus on China.

China

Buddhism entered China from northern India through Central Asian overland routes in the first century A.D. In all probability monks accompanied caravans, taking with them scriptures, relics, and Buddha images. Initially the propagation of Buddhism must have been difficult both because of the need to translate Indian Sanskrit texts into Chinese and because Confucianism was the dominant ideology of the Han dynasty (206 B.C.–A.D. 220). In Southeast Asia, Buddhism had not encountered advanced cultures and religions, but in China Confucianism and Taoism had already developed systematic world views and ethical systems. Fortunately for Indian Buddhism, Taoism provided a compatible helpmate. Philosophically, several Chinese Taoist terms were similar in meaning to Buddhist concepts. On the level of practice, both Taoists and Buddhists had a nonsacrificial ritual and both also practiced meditation.

As in other Asian countries, the popular fortunes of Buddhism in China depended in part on the support of the ruling classes. In northern China, from the fall of the Han dynasty (A.D. 220) until the beginning of the Sui dynasty (A.D. 589), Turkestan and Tibetan rulers often found it convenient to support Buddhism in place of the state Confucianism of the Han. Since monasteries were under the control of the state, they were sometimes used to carry out government policy. Also, monks skilled in the occult art of prediction often acted as advisors to rulers. State support of Buddhism was also responsible for the magnificent Buddha rock sculptures at Yun-kang and Lung-men.

In southern China, on the other hand, a more sophisticated, literary type of Buddhism developed known as "gentry Buddhism." Here some of the major lines of synthesis between Taoist and Buddhist thought developed. By the time China was reunited under the Sui dynasty in 589, Buddhism had become so popular that the emperor decided it was the appropriate ideology to unite the Chinese and non-Chinese populations of the country.

The establishment of a religion within a particular culture seems to go through several stages. In the case of China, the first stage was one of translation of texts and the establishment of a base among the ruling elite as well as the common people.

The second stage—the flowering of sinicized Buddhist schools and sects—occurred during the T'ang dynasty (618–907). The three most important sects that developed in this period were (1) the Pure Land, which emphasized faith in the Buddha Amitabha (Japanese: Amida) and rebirth in his heaven of the Pure Land; (2) T'ien-tai (Japanese: Tendai), which offered a unique synthesis of Buddhist texts, philosophical ideas, and practices; and (3) the Ch'an (Japanese: Zen), which emphasized meditation as a method for the intuitive realization of one's innate Buddha nature.

One can argue that too much material success and prosperity leads to the inevitable downfall of a religion. It becomes too involved in worldly affairs, thereby losing sight of its spiritual intent and meaning. Such a development leads to loss of purpose, to corruption, and perhaps to persecution. In the case of Chinese Buddhism, such an end came in 845. As an institution Buddhism had acquired an immense amount of economic, political, and social power. It had gained the envy and ire of both Confucianists and Taoists. In 845 an anti-Buddhist imperial edict led to the destruction of 4,600 monasteries and 40,000 temples and shrines and the return of 260,000 monks and nuns to lay

22

life. While Buddhism in China was not destroyed completely in the middle of the ninth century and continued to influence the course of Buddhism in other parts of East Asia, this date marks the beginning of the third stage, the decline of Chinese Buddhism. Today, Buddhism has been disestablished by China's rulers (see *Religion in China* in this series).

Japan and Korea

In Japan and Korea the development of Buddhism follows somewhat the same stages outlined for China: the period of establishment and assimilation, of flowering and creative development, and of decline. In Japan the Nara period (710–788) and the Heian, or Kyoto, period (794–1191) witnessed the transplanting of Buddhism on Japanese soil from China through Korea and the establishment of strong Buddhist institutions. The three major Chinese sects—Pure Land, Tendai, and Zen—underwent notable changes in Korea but especially in Japan. As in China, state support of Buddhism by the Japanese ruling classes helped to account for its rapid development and popularity.

The great creative period of Japanese Buddhism was the Kamakura (1192–1336). It was a time of political transition and is sometimes called the feudal period of Japanese history. Three of that country's most brilliant and energetic religious figures emerged at that time: (1) Dogen, the founder of the Soto Zen sect; (2) Shinran, the founder of the Jodo Shin Shu, or True Pure Land, sect; and (3) Nichiren, the founder of the Nichiren sect. Each of these traditions has had a significant impact on Japanese religious life. Of the three, the True Pure Land sect claims the largest number of adherents, although Zen has been culturally more important. One of the Nichiren sects has received attention in the past few years through an aggressive and politically active lay group known as the Soka Gakkai. Although Buddhism continues to be an important religious and cultural force in Japan, most Japanese today tend to characterize themselves and their country as secular.

Zen Buddhism for many Americans is nearly synonymous with Japanese culture. The tea ceremony, stone gardens, flower arranging, landscape paintings, haiku poetry—these and many other elements of Japanese culture are in some way or another associated with Zen. The martial arts such as swordsmanship, archery, and judo are also a part of this picture. In short, many Japanese cultural elements and aesthetic expressions have been mediated or filtered through Zen. Zen has been a valuable means of cultural transmission between China and Japan, and the Zen imprint has been left on the Japanese cultural and artistic expressions mentioned above. Currently, Zen is again serving as a vehicle of cultural transmission, this time between Japan and the United States.

To be sure, Zen Buddhism has its aesthetic and artistic dimension as do all religious traditions. Yet, as the name Zen indicates, it focuses on mental development, or meditation. This aspect of the Zen tradition has captured the imagination and, indeed, the allegiance of a growing number of Americans. At present there are over sixty Zen meditation centers throughout the United States. A variety of Zen traditions from Japan and Korea are followed here, with the Rinzai (Chinese: Lin-chi) being the best known.

Will Buddhism ever become a major religion in America? Perhaps not. However, since the end of World War II, many Americans have been becoming increasingly aware of the relevance of the teachings of the Buddha and the value of certain Buddhist practices. The influence of Zen can be seen in the poetry of Gary Snyder and the art of Will Peterson, and increasing interest in Buddhism has been shown by such notable Christian spiritual leaders as Thomas Merton, the late Trappist monk, and such Protestant theologians as John Cobb.

Part II

The Teachings of Buddhism

Many Westerners believe that the Buddha's teachings are mystical, ascetic, and otherworldly. This is far from the truth, however. Rather, the fundamental purpose of the Buddha's teachings is to resolve the deep sense of dissatisfaction (unease and suffering) that most people experience at some time or another in their lives. In fact, the appeal of the Buddha's teachings throughout the ages has been just that: a way to resolve life's dilemmas, to overcome its sorrow, to gain an unbounded sense of freedom and peace. It is the purpose of Part II to investigate the varied teachings of Buddhism about the human condition and the ways that condition can be improved.

As indicated in Part I, Buddhism had a long period of historical development in India, Southeast Asia, and East Asia. Buddhist doctrines as well as institutional and cultural forms have undergone various changes in the process of development, and, as a result, Buddhist teachings vary from country to country. For example, a Japanese Buddhist who is a member of the Japanese Pure Land sect (Jodo Shin Shu) will affirm a set of teachings different from those of the Buddhist from Sri Lanka who is a member of the Theravada school. And both of them will talk about their religious beliefs in terms different from those used by the Buddhist monk from Katmandu, Nepal, who is a member of the Thunderbolt tradition (Vajrayana). By comparison, the religious beliefs of a Roman Catholic from a village in Brazil, an Orthodox monk from Mount Athos in Greece, and a devout Southern Baptist from Alabama would also differ radically. Yet, just as such a diverse group of Christians would affirm some common teachings, so also can common elements of belief be found among Buddhists from different traditions. What, then, are those basic Buddhist teachings? Part II will examine these commonly held beliefs before moving on to some of the more distinctive teachings of the two great divisions of Buddhism—the Theravada and the Mahayana.

THE CORE TEACHINGS OF BUDDHISM

For all Buddhist traditions the Buddha Sakyamuni (meaning the *muni,* or sage, of the Sakya clan) is revered as an enlightened person whose message was responsible for founding the Buddhist tradition in the sixth century B.C. In Buddhist terminology, Sakyamuni, or Siddhartha Gautama (his given and family names), "set in motion the wheel of truth." Most fundamental to Sakyamuni's teaching or law, which Buddhists call *dharma,* is the belief that few people put forth the effort necessary to understand the world as it really is. Most people live out a lifetime that has an unreal or illusory quality about it. They see their lives and the world around them to be one thing when, in fact, it is something else. Using Western science as an analogy, most people see the world in seventeenth-century Newtonian terms rather than the terms of modern physics growing out of Einstein's theory of relativity.

From a Buddhist standpoint people's perceptions are governed by the obvious, visible, superficial aspects of life. People overlook the essential, real, and true. All forms of Buddhist teaching aim at overcoming the superficial and attaining insight into the true or real nature of existence. An ancient Indian text exclaims: "From the unreal lead me to the real; from nonexistence lead me to existence." This is precisely the intent of the teachings of Buddhism regardless of school or tradition.

Do Buddhists agree about the content of this much-prized wisdom? In general terms they do. This wisdom is based upon the understanding that the primary characteristic of existence is change, flux, impermanence. The teaching of the Buddha is both as simple and as difficult as that: all things in this world are subject to change. The legend of the Buddha's encounter with four types of people, discussed in Part I, offers a graphic illustration of this teaching—namely, that one's life inevitably falls victim to illness, old age, and finally death. Life is constantly subject to change just as the world is one in process and not static. In an episode from the Buddhist texts of the Theravada tradition, one of the Buddha's disciples was confronted by a questioner who asked, "What is your teacher's *dharma* (teaching)?" His simple reply was, "All things are subject to change."

A Western response to this central teaching of Buddhism might be, "Well, what's so significant about that? Of course everyone knows that the world is always changing." Ah yes, but does everyone *live* in terms of that insight? Do people not rather build their lives on the assumption that the world is stable and permanent rather than changing and in process? Do you remember, for example, how the United States fought in World War II to "make the world safe for democracy"? Or, of more recent memory, do you recall how people responded to the energy crises of 1974 by saying, "America will be self-sufficient in energy by 1980!" Finally, in front of a brand-new, totally enclosed shopping mall there was a large billboard which read, "ETERNAL SPRING. Grand Opening. . . ." Regardless of what they know about the processes of nature, the lessons of history, and the whimsical quality of their own lives, do Americans not believe (or at least want to believe) that the United States can make the world safe for democracy forever, or that they can permanently solve the energy problem without changing their life-style, or that they can construct an eternal spring? The Buddha taught that people live under such false expectations and that, therefore, they live unreal lives.

For the Buddhist, ignorance or unwillingness to accept the continually changing nature of the world creates serious moral problems. The stubborn insistence on getting ahead even at the expense of others, the drive to defend self-interest, the accumulation of wealth and material benefits far beyond human needs—all result from the belief that life has an everlasting quality. People really do act on the belief that being first in their class will make them truly happy, or that to be really satisfied all they need is a new car, new house, and so on. Buddhism teaches, first, that such goals are like a mirage. Once they have been attained or acquired, the condition of happiness and well-being that was sought soon disappears. Second, acting in terms of such erroneous beliefs makes people greedy, prompts hatred, and engenders self-destructive ambition. The social consequences of such personal traits, furthermore, lead to disruptive interpersonal relationships, social disharmony, and war.

The Buddhist teaching is a path, or *marga,* to eliminate the causes of such personal and social ills. Buddhism assumes that by understanding these causes people can overcome them, and that by overcoming the causes of unhappiness and suffering they will achieve a state of supreme bliss known by the term *Nirvana.* The Buddha's teaching aims to dispel ignorance—the mirage that a condition of material well-being sufficient to satisfy the deepest longings of human beings can be created in this life. Once people acknowledge—not simply as a logical conclusion but as an experientially and deeply felt truth—that, for example, "eternal springs" cannot be produced by air conditioning, then their orientation to life changes. Ambitions become less self-centered with the realization that the competitive drive to be first can be destructive or at best temporarily satisfying, and that incessant desires and petty hatreds cause suffering. In short, once people squarely face the impermanent and changing nature of the ego, they

27

become less ego-defensive. Precisely in coming to a deeper understanding of themselves and the nature of the world around them, they become more open, more tolerant, and more loving. In accepting themselves and others as they really are, they discover a new peace and a new freedom.

THE FOUR NOBLE TRUTHS

The above characterization of the core teachings of Buddhism is a very general and somewhat Westernized one. All Buddhists, however, whether Burmese, Tibetan, or Japanese, would find this description compatible with their own tradition's symbols and doctrinal systems. Before passing on to a few of the most distinctive teachings of the Theravada tradition, which still flourishes today in Sri Lanka, Burma, Thailand, Cambodia, and Laos, we need to examine more specifically the teachings of the Buddha as found in his first public teaching, or First Sermon, known as "setting the wheel of truth in motion." According to the Buddhist tradition this sermon, delivered to five of his first disciples at the Deer Park in Sarnath near present-day Benares, India, represents the Buddha's first teaching after his enlightenment. It is found in its complete form in most anthologies of Buddhist scripture in translation. Here is a portion of it.

> Thus I have heard: at one time the Blessed One dwelt at Benares at Isipatana in the Deer Park. There he addressed the five monks:
>
> "These two extremes, monks, are not to be practiced by one who has gone forth from the world. What are the two? That conjoined with the passions and luxury, which is low, vulgar, common, ignoble, and useless; and that conjoined with self-torture, which is painful, ignoble, and useless. Avoiding these two extremes the Blessed One has gained the enlightenment of the Middle Path, which produces insight and knowledge, and leads to calm, to higher knowledge, enlightenment, Nirvana.
>
> "And what, monks, is the Middle Path . . . ? It is the noble Eightfold Path: namely, right view, right intention, right speech, right action, right livelihood, right effort, right mindfulness, right concentration. . . .
>
> "Now this, monks, is the noble truth of pain [*dukkha*]: birth is painful, old age is painful, sickness is painful, death is painful, sorrow, lamentation, dejection, and despair are painful. Contact with unpleasant things is painful, not getting what one wishes is painful. In short the five components of existence are painful.
>
> "Now this, monks, is the noble truth of the cause of pain: the craving, which tends to rebirth, combined with pleasure and lust,

finding pleasure here and there; namely, the craving for passion, the craving for existence, the craving for non-existence.

"Now this, monks, is the noble truth of the cessation of pain, the cessation without a remainder of craving, the abandonment, forsaking, release, non-attachment.

"Now this, monks, is the noble truth of the path that leads to the cessation of pain: this is the noble Eightfold Path [see above]."[1]

This part of the First Sermon contains one of the frequently used summaries of early Buddhist teaching—the Four Noble Truths and the Eightfold Path. As you read this selection, did you notice the repetitive style of the text? What do you think is the reason for this kind of literary style? You are correct if you guessed that it grew out of oral tradition. These texts were memorized for centuries before they were written down. Indeed, even after assuming written form they continued to be memorized. Even today it is reported that there is a Burmese monk in Mandalay who can repeat the entire canon of Theravada Buddhism by heart!

The First Sermon emphasizes the Buddhist teaching that suffering, the fundamental human problem, is caused by attachment to things and by the craving accompanying this attachment. The way to supreme happiness is the elimination of attachment. Merely thinking about one's problems does not get rid of them. One needs to understand their roots and then act on that understanding. Thus in the First Sermon the Four Noble Truths include the Eightfold Path, practical instructions about the way to solve life's suffering and pain. This path is called "the middle way" between the extremes of asceticism and luxurious living. The Buddha's own life dramatizes the middle way character of Buddhism in his rejection of both the privileged life of a prince and the mortifications of the flesh as an ascetic. Buddhism is not to be seen as a world-renouncing religion. True, the Buddhist is antimaterialistic and denies that ultimate happiness derives from worldly rewards; however, the Buddha was just as critical of the extreme of world-renouncing asceticism as he was of an "eat, drink, and be merry" philosophy of life.

This middle way character of Buddhism manifests itself in all of its schools but is probably best known to Westerners in its Japanese Zen form. Many are the tales of a Zen master's impatience with a disciple's inability to understand that the middle way does not mean the rejection of the things of this world but rather the ability to see them for what they really are, that is, to see their true, or their Buddha, nature. The famous Ten Ox Herding pictures illustrate the middle way nature of Zen Buddhism. Their message is a simple one: the quest for the lost ox leads home, just as Nirvana, or enlightenment, is to be found where you are right now.

The particular path charted in the First Sermon is the Eightfold Path: right view, right thought, right speech, right action, right livelihood, right effort, right mindfulness, right concentration. Without delving into a detailed analysis of the Eightfold Path, it is important to note that for all Buddhists the path consists of three major parts: (1) moral virtue or right ethical conduct, (2) a mentally disciplined or meditative life, and (3) the realization of a higher or transcendental wisdom or truth. It can be seen, for example, how "right livelihood" is part of ethical behavior, "right mindfulness" comes under mental discipline, and "right view" is part of the attainment of a transcendental wisdom. Furthermore, in all schools of Buddhism these three aspects of the Buddhist path presuppose one another. Thus the morally virtuous person has achieved wisdom, and this wisdom presupposes a mentally disciplined life. As will be seen in Part III, although the various schools of Buddhism differ in form and practice, all of them have adapted and developed ethical norms, devotional practices, and meditative disciplines. In relation to Western religious practice, meditation stands out as being especially unique. In the last few years American Roman Catholics have experimented with Buddhist meditation as a means to deepen their own spirituality. Thomas Merton, the well-known Trappist mystic, found Zen Buddhism and Taoism to be of great religious inspiration. Unfortunately, his untimely death in 1968 cut short his development of even further insight derived from Buddhism.

As the second Noble Truth points out, craving or thirst leads not only to suffering and unhappiness but to reexistence or rebecoming (*samsara*). You may recall from the story of Satien's ordination in the Prologue that the major belief behind the ordination was that of rebirth, or reexistence, coupled with the law of *karma*. These two teachings are found in all Buddhist traditions, although the interpretation may vary. In general, *karma* theory says every action and even intention has a consequence for good or for evil. *Karma* extends back into the past and forward into the future through the concept of reexistence (*samsara*). *Samsara* is the belief that this particular lifetime is but a part of a series of existences and that the shape of present life is conditioned by past intentions and actions. Theoretically, according to the doctrinal teachings of Theravada Buddhism, no one can escape his or her *karma*, since each person is nothing more than the product of his or her past. Only Nirvana, a goal many lifetimes away, is beyond the power of *karma*. Yet, in practice, most forms of Buddhism developed various means for easing the burden of *karma* if not actually canceling it out. Satien's ordination was a good example of how the merit of an act performed by someone else may bring about karmic benefit to another.

Karma theory provides the world with a kind of spiritual justice. In Buddhism the dilemma of Job, or why the righteous suffer and the unrighteous or unjust prosper, is answered in terms of *karma* and *samsara*. While it may not be possible to explain precisely why a righteous person suffers in this life, Buddhists believe that such suffering reflects bad *karma* (i.e., unjust acts) at some time in the past. Such an answer may not satisfy a Western mind; nonetheless, it avoids Job's dilemma which stems from a belief in a righteous God.

This discussion of the First Sermon has pointed out a few of the commonly held views of Buddhists: (1) that Buddhism is not world renouncing but is rather antimaterialistic; (2) that in Buddhism, theory and practice are interrelated; (3) that suffering *(dukkha)* is rooted in sensory craving and attachment; and (4) that attachment is fundamentally a condition or state of bondage to a wheel of reexistence, or rebirth, operating according to an inevitable law of moral justice *(karma)*. The excerpt from the First Sermon also points to a state beyond bondage—one of emancipation, freedom, and wisdom, that is, Nirvana. All Buddhist traditions uphold such a goal, although interpretations vary. Nirvana will be discussed later when the teachings of the Theravada and the Mahayana are treated in more detail. Before that discussion, another widely held theory must be examined, the doctrine of Dependent Co-origination.

DEPENDENT CO-ORIGINATION

The Buddhist concept of Dependent Co-origination is a very early formulation or symbolization of the truism that life continually changes and that it is an interdependent, ongoing process. While the concept was modified during its historical development, it came to be formalized by all Buddhist schools as the twelve-stage cycle depicted on page 34.

The principle behind this cycle, or circle, of interconnected parts is stated as follows: "when this is, that is; when this arises, that arises; when this is not, that is not; when this ceases to be, that ceases to be." Within the specific conceptual framework of the cycle of Dependent Co-origination, this principle of mutually conditioned existence can be stated as follows:

1. Through ignorance are conditioned volitional actions.
2. Through volitional actions is conditioned consciousness.
3. Through consciousness are conditioned mental and physical phenomena.
4. Through mental and physical phenomena are conditioned the six components of one's existence (i.e., the five physical sense organs and the mind).
5. Through the six components is conditioned the contact the mind and body have with the world.
6. Through this contact is conditioned sensation.
7. Through sensation are conditioned desire, thirst, and craving.
8. Through desire is conditioned clinging.
9. Through clinging is conditioned the very process of becoming, i.e., life through the cycles of reexistence.
10. Through the process of becoming is conditioned birth.
11-12. Through the process of birth are conditioned decay, death, lamentation, pain, etc.[2]

This particular depiction of the Dependent Co-origination is taken from a typical Tibetan design. Throughout Tibet, Nepal, Sikkim, and Bhutan, this design is reproduced in paintings on temple walls, on long hanging scrolls, or *tankas,* and on copper plate reliefs. As this picture shows, the outer rim of the wheel portrays the twelve aspects of the cycle, describing life as a constant, interdependent process. In the inner hub there are three animals—a snake, a pig, and a rooster—symbolizing human hatred, ignorance, and greed. These qualities, the "ills that mortal flesh is heir to," keep the wheel of existence in motion. Once these qualities are eliminated, the wheel ceases or, in the terminology of Buddhist thought, life's ills *(dukkha)* are overcome and peace and freedom (Nirvana) are attained. The scenes in the interior part of the wheel represent various states into which a person might be reborn. Numerous lifetimes of good deeds are rewarded by rebirth in the realms of the gods *(devas)*, while a legacy of bad deeds may result in one's rebirth in the realm of the demons and "hungry ghosts" (see lower left-hand quadrant).

The Buddhist cosmology reflected in this depiction of the wheel of Dependent Co-origination was adapted into the Buddhist tradition from Indian Brahmanic thought. Without going into great detail, it is important to note that this cosmos is divided into three major realms: demonic, human, and heavenly. As was the case in medieval Christianity (and, indeed, in some forms of Christianity today), the heavens and hells are seen as rewards or punishments for good or bad behavior. The reward of heaven and the punishment of hell play an important role in popular piety. As Westerners, we may not find such teachings very appealing; yet we cannot hope to understand Buddhism as practiced in Asia today by ignoring them. They are an essential part of the lived tradition.

The belief that life is a process is not really foreign to Westerners. Much of both modern science and modern philosophy is rooted in such a view. Think for a moment of the significance of Darwinian evolutionary theory for the understanding of biology or of Einstein's theory of relativity for the understanding of modern physics. One of the most important modern philosophers, Alfred North Whitehead, founded a school of philosophy known as "process philosophy." This is not to say that the Buddhist view of existence as one of interdependent elements in the process of constant change is the same as that of Darwin, or Einstein, or Whitehead; yet the general perspective among them is not dissimilar. Thus the rather strange picture of the wheel of Dependent Co-origination should not be viewed as being totally foreign to views of the world developed in the ancient or modern west.

This section on the teachings of Buddhism began with a general interpretation of the main thrust of Buddhist thought. Next, more traditional Buddhist concepts were analyzed by using the Buddha's First Sermon and the symbol of the wheel of Dependent Co-origination. Now, the following sections will treat some of the particular doctrinal emphases found in the two divisions of Buddhism known as the Theravada and the Mahayana. While all of even the most important teachings of the wide scope of Buddhism cannot be covered here, these sections serve to develop insight into some of them. The Bibliography will facilitate further study.

THERAVADA: THE TEACHINGS OF THE ELDERS

As learned in Part I, the doctrines of Buddhism developed through a series of councils held specifically for the purpose of organizing and ordering the teachings attributed to the Buddha and later elaborations on them. One result of these meetings was agreement on the texts considered to be orthodox for particular schools of Buddhism. This same process of definition continued in other parts of Asia and continues still.

In the Theravada tradition, which came to predominate in Southeast Asia, a keen interest in establishing an orthodox scriptural canon arose. Generally, scholars agree that its major segments were estab-

lished by the third century B.C. at the council held under the aegis of King Asoka. This canon had a long oral history, not being written down until the first century A.D. during the reign of Vattagamani in Sri Lanka. The doctrines of Theravada Buddhism are contained in its scriptures, commentaries on these scriptures, and various expositions that have been produced throughout the history of this tradition. Such a developmental sequence is similar to Christianity. In both cases there was a founder who was perceived as a wise teacher, the development of a scriptural canon, the definition of correct doctrine through a series of councils, and the spread of various teachings. This brief historical observation about the formation of Buddhist teaching is made in order to point out that the teachings discussed in this section presuppose a complex historical development. The following discussion of Theravada teachings focuses on (1) the role of analysis in Theravada doctrine, (2) the nature of the self, (3) the concept of sainthood, and (4) the nature of the final goal, or Nirvana.

The Role of Analysis

The particular school of Indian Buddhism to which the Theravada tradition is probably most indebted was called the School of Analysis. Nolan P. Jacobson, a contemporary American philosopher of religion, has written a fascinating book about Theravada Buddhist thought called *Buddhism: The Religion of Analysis*. What does it mean to say

A painting of the Wheel of Becoming, Tibetan style.

that the Theravada is a religion of analysis? In answering this question one of the major perspectives of this important Buddhist tradition can be established.

Early Buddhism understood human suffering *(dukkha)* to be caused by ignorance of the real nature of the world. This blindness was caused, in turn, by a dependence on the senses. It is a vicious circle: a lack of understanding is caused by a blind sensory attachment, and a blind attachment is caused by a lack of understanding. A well-known Theravada text puts it this way:

> Everything, O Brothers, is on fire. How is everything on fire? The eye is on fire, visible objects are on fire, the faculty of the eye is on fire, the sense of the eye is on fire, and also the sensation, whether pleasant or unpleasant or both, which arises from the sense of sight is on fire. With what is it on fire? With the fire of passion, of hate, of illusion is it on fire. . . .[3]

The text continues by saying the ear and sounds, the nose and scents, the tongue and tastes, the body and objects of touch, mind and mental objects are all on fire with passion, hate, illusion, and with birth, old age, death, grief, lamentations, suffering, sorrow, and despair. Buddhism, then, challenges its followers to overcome twin enemies—sensory attachment and ignorance. It proposes to accomplish this end by wisdom attained through understanding and mental training.

As a simple example, people may react to their environment in two basic ways. One way is to change the environment. Clearly, this is the way of Western technology. Another way more consonant with Buddhism is to change one's attitude toward or relationship with the environment. To illustrate this second approach, think for a moment about one of those times when you felt essentially negative about your environment—for example, "It's cold and snowy outside. What a mess!"—and when the reaction of a friend was positive—"Say, it's snowing outside. Let's go sledding!" The difference was one of attitude and reaction. The Buddhist approaches human suffering *(dukkha)* by pointing out that the nature of the world is conditioned by the mind. That is, through right understanding and mental training, a new relationship to the world can be constructed; and in the process of changing mental attitude, the environment is changed as well. In the words of the *Dhammapada,* probably the most famous of all Buddhist scriptures:

> All that we are is the result of what we have thought: it is founded on our thoughts, it is made up of our thoughts. If a man speaks or

acts with an evil thought, pain follows him, as the wheel follows the foot of the ox that draws the carriage.

All that we are is the result of what we have thought: it is founded on our thoughts, it is made up of our thoughts. If a man speaks or acts with a pure thought, happiness follows him, like a shadow that never leaves him.[4]

Right understanding has a moral consequence. What people know affects what they are and that, in turn, affects the way they act in the world. Sadly, American education in recent years has tended to overlook the moral consequences of knowledge, an insight central to the Buddhist approach to life.

Do good deeds result from good thoughts? Do bad habits lead to bad deeds? What does it mean to say that understanding and knowledge condition not only the way people relate to their environment but the way their environment relates to them? Two illustrations may help to answer this question. Suppose that you are going to the beach for an afternoon swim. After an hour or so you notice a shark fin jutting above the water. Taking no chances you get out and inform the lifeguard who in turn puts in a call for an aerial sighting. Three dangerous sharks are observed and the beach is cleared, probably averting at least one serious injury. Your knowledge of the true situation on the beach that afternoon led you to act in such a way that your life and the lives of others were spared. Buddhism perceives the consequences of right understanding to be as dramatically significant in a religious or spiritual sense.

A second illustration answers the question in a slightly different way. In many primitive societies the knowledge of conception and birth is rudimentary at best. Consequently, what people in some parts of the world take for granted in the areas of birth control and personal hygiene is unknown in these primitive societies and therefore not practiced. Action is conditioned largely by the taboos surrounding the mystery of conception and birth. While no student of such cultures would deny the meaningfulness of the myths and practices surrounding these important events, knowledge of the biological facts would have changed, and indeed in some cases has changed, many behavioral patterns. Similarly, the Theravada tradition offers an analysis of life which aims not only to describe the way things are but to produce changes in behavior and action in the world. This analysis will now be examined in more detail.

One of the first points to keep in mind is that objective understanding minimizes blind, subjective attachment. The assumption here is a simple one: namely, the analysis of a problem, issue, or situation gives an objective perspective on it. As an example, you have probably had the experience where you have become intensely angry—indeed, so angry that you "couldn't see straight." You might even have acted on that anger to the injury of someone else or yourself. Later, when your anger cooled down, you probably not only regretted your rash response but, by analyzing the causes of your anger, either dispelled the feeling or transformed it into a more positive emotion.

One of the stories in the Theravada texts illustrates this teaching by relating an amorous adventure of a group of courtiers. One day they decided to go for a swim. The married courtiers took their wives. One of the unmarried young men invited a courtesan to go along. While they were all swimming in the buff, the courtesan hid the others' clothes and ran away. Discovering the trick, the courtiers took off in pursuit only to pass by the Buddha on their way. In anger (and probably in embarrassment as well) the young men inquired whether he had seen the courtesan in question. With this opening, the Buddha proceeded to ask whether a search for the meaning of their lives (i.e., the nature of the self) would not be a more worthwhile pursuit. The Buddha's query forced the young courtiers to stop, to consider their situation in a new light, and in their embarrassment to see the folly of such frivolous living. The Buddha's wise query prompted a kind of analytical distance on a previously uncontemplated problem.

The Self

The Theravada tradition argues that the locus of analytical or objective distance rests in the understanding that people have of themselves as persons. Of course we must know the nature of the world around us, but it is even more critical to understand ourselves as we really are. For Buddhism, the human problem is the most important religious issue. Who are we? Are we like the young courtiers running around helter-skelter in the woods with no clue as to who we are or what we are looking for? Buddhism assumes that we are—that we are too busy in the pursuit of our own pleasures (and pains) to pause to examine seriously the questions "Who am I?" and "What am I doing in the world?" In particular, the Theravada tradition argues that most people have a totally inaccurate understanding of their true nature. Consequently, the first task is to correct this false view and in the process move to a new self-understanding. This twofold process is most often characterized by the term not-self (an-atta).

The Theravada concept of not-self is one of its most important teachings and at the same time perhaps the least understood. The Pali term *an-atta* translates literally as "not" *(an)* "self" *(atta)*. Because the word itself is a negation, several Western scholars argue that Buddhism must be a negative religion. This, in the author's opinion, is a fundamental misunderstanding, for the Theravada use of negative terms has a positive intent. In the following passage from a text called *The Questions of King Milinda,* a conversation takes place between a Buddhist monk, Nagasena, and Milinda (or Menander), the ruler of a Greco-Indian state in northwestern India in the first century A.D. In one passage the Venerable Nagasena speaks to the king as follows:

Your majesty, you are a delicate prince and if, your majesty, you walk in the middle of the day on hot sandy ground and walk over rough gravel your feet become sore, your body tired, the mind is oppressed, and the body-consciousness suffers. Pray, did you come on foot or did you ride?

Bhante (Reverend Sir), I did not go on foot but came in a chariot.

Your majesty, if you came in a chariot, identify the chariot. Pray, your majesty, is the pole the chariot?

Nay, verily, Bhante.

Is the axle the chariot?

Nay, verily, Bhante.

Are the wheels the chariot?

Nay, verily, Bhante.

Is the chariot-body the chariot?

Nay, verily, Bhante.

Is the banner-staff the chariot?

Nay, verily, Bhante. . . .

Pray, your majesty, are the pole, axle, wheels, chariot-body, and banner-staff unitedly the chariot?

Nay, verily, Bhante.

Is it, then, your majesty, something else beside pole, axle, wheels, chariot-body, and banner-staff which is the chariot?

Nay, verily, Bhante.

Your majesty, although I question you very closely, I fail to identify the chariot. Truly, your majesty, the word chariot is a mere empty sound.

Milinda replies, "Bhante Nagasena, you speak the truth. The word 'chariot' is but a way of counting, a term, appellation, convenient designation, the name for pole, axle, wheels, chariot-body, and banner-staff."

Thoroughly well, your majesty, do you understand a chariot. In exactly the same way, your majesty, in regard to me, I, Nagasena, am but a way of counting, a term, appellation, convenient designation, mere name for the hair of my head, hair of my body, brain of my head, form, sensation, perception, predispositions, and consciousness. But in the absolute sense there is no ego to be found here.[5]

What is it that the not-self teaching denies? As Nagasena states, there is no underlying self, no soul or substructure beyond the components of physical and mental life. Theravada Buddhism devised several ways of analyzing the dual aspects of the mental and physical coordinates of personal existence. The above dialogue is, in its own right, a kind of analysis by way of analogy. At least as the text presents the situation, the chariot analogy that the individual is but a collection of component parts with no "self" or soul to be found was convincing. King Milinda departs the scene aware of this truth.

The Theravada tradition evolved more elaborate and technical analyses than this argument from analogy. The preceding dialogue illustrates the idea in its most simple form. Elsewhere, as in the First Sermon, the not-self teaching is part of the discussion of the five components or aspects of individual existence. These five are (1) form (or body), (2) sensation, (3) perception, (4) predispositions, and (5) consciousness. Another very naturalistic model lists thirty-two elements, including the hair of the head, hair of the body, and so on. Still other classifications found in the Theravada scriptures become more and more elaborate until in one of the later, more philosophical texts the writers arrived at a list of over a hundred bodily and mental components. These analyses become so interminably long that the reader may lose sight of their dual purpose: to provide analytical distance on the otherwise thoughtless involvement in the pursuits of the world, and to convince the reader or listener that ordinary understanding of the self is false. As difficult as it may be to fully comprehend, the not-self teaching and the analytical method employed to convey that teaching are essential to the Theravada understanding of the basic human problem and its solution. The passage from *The Questions of King Milinda* reveals that the not-self teaching denies the existence of a soul or a self beyond the body, feelings, perceptions, will, and consciousness. How do Theravada Buddhists arrive at this denial?

The not-self teaching reinforces the Theravada position that the effort to analyze some problems is spiritually edifying but that analysis of other problems can be a waste of time or even misleading. For example, trying to determine whether or not there is a soul and trying to define the self or the ego are two of those problems that "tend not to edification." While such problems may be interesting to think about, nevertheless, they divert one's energies away from the sort of analysis that leads to wisdom. In a dialogue with one of his followers— Malunkyaputta by name—the Buddha uses an oft-quoted analogy to illustrate the uselessness of speculating about such questions as whether the world is eternal, the soul and the body are identical, or the saint exists after death. To engage in these questions is, according to the Buddha,

> ". . . as if a man had been wounded by an arrow thickly smeared with poison, and his friends and companions, his relatives and kinsfolk, were to procure for him a physician or surgeon; and the sick man were to say, 'I will not have this arrow taken out until I have learned whether the man who wounded me belonged to the warrior caste, or to the Brahman caste, or to the agricultural caste or the servant caste or to what clan he belongs or whether the man who wounded me was tall, or short, or of middle height or whether the man who wounded me was black, or dusky, or a yellow skin. . . ."

> "That man would die, Malunkyaputta, without ever having learned this."[6]

Similarly, speculation about the nature of the self is dangerous, for it prevents direct confrontation with feelings, perceptions, volitions, and thoughts. It throws a kind of shadow-person over the screen of vision, thereby distorting it. Shadows or images are seen rather than things as they really are. Theravada Buddhism tries to cut through those images and shadows. It moves out of a make-believe world into reality by its insistence upon the proper perception of the situations that are encountered in life.

The not-self teaching also serves to emphasize the Buddhist goal of nonattachment. Logically speaking, how can selfishness, greed, lust, hatred, and similar qualities exist if analysis has eliminated the focal motivating point (i.e., the self) from such passions? Understanding, even-mindedness, and true compassion arise through the practical elimination of ego-centeredness. People are able to act freed from the subjective biases, prejudices, and defenses of ego hang-ups only when they are totally aware of themselves and their environment. Such awareness means, in the Theravada analysis, the elimination of the ego as an artificial construct produced through ignorance.

This study of Theravada thought has thus far examined the nature of the concept of not-self *(an-atta)* and the moral consequences of the method of analytical distance which go along with it. An understanding of these teachings will be of help in examining the Theravada concept of the saint and the nature of the highest goal, Nirvana.

The Saint

What is a saint? In the Roman Catholic church a saint must be canonized, and to be so honored certain qualifications must be met such as the certification of miracles attributed to him or her and so on. But in a general sense, a saint is ordinarily thought of as someone qualified by an unusual wisdom, kindness, and extraordinary compassion and spirituality. Such traits would characterize a saintly person in almost any religion; however, each religion has its own descriptions of sainthood. The *Dhammapada* gives the following characterization of the Buddhist saint, or *arahat* ("worthy one").

There is no suffering for him who has finished his journey and abandoned grief, who has freed himself on all sides and thrown off all fetters.

They move with well collected thoughts . . .; like swans who have left their lake, they leave their house and home. . . . He who has no riches, . . . whose appetites are stilled, who is not absorbed in enjoyment, who has perceived unconditioned freedom (Nirvana), his path is difficult to understand, like that of the birds of the air.

Even the gods envy him whose senses, like horses well broken in by the drive, have been subdued, who is free from pride, and free from appetites; such a one . . . is tolerant like the earth, or like a threshold; he is like a lake without mud; no new births await him. His thought is quiet, quiet are his word and deed when he has obtained freedom through true knowledge. . . .

A guardian of the entrance to a Buddhist temple in Thailand.

The man who is free from credulity, but knows the uncreated [Nirvana], who has cut all ties, removed all temptations, renounced all desires, he is the greatest of men.[7]

The Theravada saint *(arahat)*, then, is one who has overcome the fetters or attachment to purely worldly pursuits, who has perceived unconditioned freedom (Nirvana), who is tolerant and free from pride, who has overcome the power of karmic force and, therefore, of rebirth. In sum, the saint has overcome his egoism or, in the terminology of Theravada Buddhism, he is a not-self. He has negated those conditions which prevented him from realizing the full dimension of his existence; he has overcome those limitations of unthinking involvement in the world and habitual attachment; he has plumbed a depth of life that most people hardly realize exists. The *Dhammapada* likens him to a swan whose grace in flight reminded the early Indian thinkers of freedom and immortality. Most people, as Richard Bach writes in *Jonathan Livingston Seagull,* are quite content to follow along with the crowd, to do what everyone else is doing, instead of looking for deeper meaning to life. Unlike the *arahat* they are content with the superficial aspect of life and fall short not only in wisdom but in virtue. Most people have also fallen short of the realization of perfect freedom (Nirvana) and are, therefore, imperfectly tolerant, open, and compassionate. While the Theravada saint has achieved his status through his own efforts, his self-realization does not mean that he cuts himself off from others. The best example of the Buddhist saint's compassionate concern for others is the Buddha himself who chose to teach others the way to Nirvana rather than enjoying the bliss of that state only for himself.

The Final Goal

The conception of the saint in Theravada Buddhist thought cannot be discussed without also discussing the nature of the perfect freedom realized by the Buddha. Nirvana has been a troublesome idea for students of Buddhism. Just what is it? The term itself does not offer much help. Like not-self *(an-atta)*, Nirvana is a negative term. Literally, it means the "blowing out" of the flame of desire, the negation of suffering *(dukkha)*. This implies that Nirvana is not to be thought of as a place but as a total reorientation or state of being realized as a consequence of the extinction of blinding and binding attachment. Thus, at least, Nirvana implies that the kind of existence one has achieved is inconceivable in the ordinary terms of the world. As Dr. Walpola Rahula, a Sinhalese Buddhist monk and author of the excellent book *What the Buddha Taught* says, "The only reasonable reply to give to the question [What is Nirvana?] is that it can never be answered completely and satisfactorily in words, because human language is too poor to express the real nature of the Absolute Truth or Ultimate Reality which is Nirvana."[8] He goes on to say that words cannot adequately express the experience of Nirvana just as a fish has no words in its vocabulary to express the nature of the solid land. The "otherness" of the experience of Nirvana does not mean, however, that it is not discussed in the Theravada texts. Let us examine a few passages in which Nirvana is mentioned.

> Dispassion is called the Way. It is said: "Through dispassion is one freed." Yet, in meaning, all these (words: stopping, renunciation, surrender, release, lack of clinging) are synonyms for Nirvana. For, according to its ultimate meaning, Nirvana is the Aryan Truth of the stopping of suffering.[9]

> "Venerable Nagasena, things produced of *karma* are seen in the world, things produced of cause are seen, things produced of nature are seen. Tell me, what in the world is born not of *karma*, not of cause, not of nature."[10]

> There is, monks, that plane where there is neither extension nor . . . motion nor the plane of infinite space . . . nor that of neither-perception-nor-non-perception, neither this world nor another, neither the moon nor the sun. Here, monks, I say that there is no coming or going or remaining or deceasing or uprising, for this is itself without any support. . . .

> There is, monks, an unborn, not become, not made, uncompounded, and . . . because there is, . . . an escape can be shown for what is born, has become, is made, is compounded.[11]

These three passages point to different aspects of the concept of Nirvana. The first passage illustrates our initial claim about Nirvana, namely, that it is the negation of attachment and suffering *(dukkha)*. The second, a question from King Milinda, is answered, as you probably guessed, by Nirvana. Nirvana, then, is the one thing that is not caused by anything else. The third quotation pushes this idea even further. Together these passages express what Dr. Rahula pointed out: Nirvana as the Absolute Truth cannot be adequately expressed in words. Nonetheless, the term implies that there is a goal to be reached and that this goal surpasses anything experienced in this world of conventional understanding.

Is there anything comparable to the Nirvana experience in Western religious thought? Indeed there is. Both Jewish and Christian mystics have held similar ideas about God. The experience of God is beyond ordinary comprehension, because God himself is unlike anything in this world. Mystics like St. John of the Cross and Meister Eckhart expressed a profound awareness of the uniqueness of religious experience, a mystery beyond the language of most ordinary experiences. They, too, sometimes employed negative terms for the mystical experience just as Buddhists chose to use such words as Nirvana for their experience of the truth. The communication of the experience of Nirvana or of God is equally difficult. As Dr. Rahula indicated, the experience of Absolute Truth can never be completely and satisfactorily put into words.

MAHAYANA: THE GREAT VEHICLE

Part I outlined some of the historical factors in India that led to the development of that great stream of Buddhism called the Mahayana. It was also pointed out that sects within this Buddhist tradition had their greatest success in East Asia. These sects hold fairly similar philosophies, which is especially evident when some of the most popular Mahayana texts are considered. This section examines a few of those commonly held ideas, indicating relevant contrasts with the Theravada tradition. After a discussion of the general orientation of the Mahayana world view, this section moves on to consider the conception of the Buddha in this tradition, the nature of the Mahayana saint *(bodhisattva)*, and finally the concept of the universal Buddha nature. In the course of this section, various selections from Mahayana texts are examined, beginning with the most famous short scripture in the Zen sect of Mahayana Buddhism known as the *Heart Sutra* or the *Heart of the Perfection of Wisdom Sutra.*

> When the *bodhisattva* Avalokitesvara [a deity of mercy] was meditating deeply on the Perfect Wisdom by means of which one reaches the Other Shore [Nirvana], he saw clearly that the five constituents of existence were all empty, and so he was saved from all kinds of suffering and misery.
>
> Then he addressed Sariputra [one of the Buddha's favorite disciples], saying: "O Sariputra! The body is not different from emptiness and emptiness is not different from the body. The body is emptiness, and emptiness is the body.
>
> "All things are empty. They neither come into existence nor pass out of existence. They neither defile nor purify, increase nor decrease.
>
> "Therefore in emptiness there is no form, no sensation, no idea, no will, no consciousness. There is no eye, no ear, no nose, no

46

tongue, no body, no thought, and so there is no color, no sound, no odor, no taste, no contact, no mental object.

"There is neither world of sight nor world of thought and consciousness. There is neither ignorance nor termination of ignorance. There is neither old age and death nor termination of old age and death.

"There is neither suffering, nor cause of suffering, nor extinction of suffering, nor way of escape from suffering [i.e., the Four Noble Truths].

"There is neither knowledge nor attainment in knowledge.

"Because there is no attainment in knowledge, the *bodhisattvas* rely on the Perfect Wisdom by means of which one reaches the Other Shore. Their minds are freed from hindrances and obstructions.

"Because they are freed from hindrances and obstructions, they have neither fear nor dread, and they do away entirely with perverse thoughts, and finally reach Nirvana."[12]

The preceding discussion of Theravada thought shows how a conventional understanding of the world is rejected on the grounds that such a view is badly distorted or unreal. It is based on surface or superficial reactions of the senses, which fail to probe beneath surface impressions of sense objects. A more searching investigation accompanying mental training or meditative procedures reveals that sense objects, including persons, are subject to constant change and lack the permanence they only appear to have. Hence, parallel in some ways to a modern scientific analysis, the Theravadins claim that all objects in the world are composed of impermanent subparts, or components. While objects as they are ordinarily perceived do not exist, their components do. The Theravadins call these components *dharmas,* and they describe human beings in terms of various schemes of *dharmas,* for example, thirty-two bodily parts. They believe that the moral consequence of such analyses will be to reduce worldly attachment. After all, if there is no ego, how can there be egoism?

As it turned out, the school which gave rise to the Theravada became overly preoccupied with its analytical schemes. In reaction to this kind of academic philosophy, other Buddhist thinkers took the position that the Theravadins had not solved the problem of attachment but had merely substituted one kind of attachment for another. They claimed that the Theravadins had become as attached to their conceptual schemes as others were to sense objects, and by so doing had become as blinded by intellectual arrogance as ordinary people were blinded by their greed, hatred, and lust. The *Heart Sutra,* representing this new point of view which contributed to the Mahayana tradition, says, therefore, that the five components of existence (form or body, sensation, perception, volitions, and consciousness) are empty. That is, this scripture is saying that the conceptual schemes of Theravada academic scholasticism are as void of truth as the sense objects they attempted to replace. Indeed the text goes on to indicate that all concepts so dear to the earlier Buddhist scholars are void of essential truth or meaning.

Perhaps an analogy will help clarify this point. As a student, you have probably had the experience of working very hard to understand a math or physics problem and then suddenly stopping and asking yourself whether such study is worth the effort. Or perhaps you have successfully solved a long and complicated equation or paradigm only to reflect, "What's the value of what I've done?" or "Does it really make any difference in the long run?" A group of Buddhist scholars who began writing during the first two centuries A.D. asked similar questions. They wondered whether the philosophies of these older scholars really made any difference spiritually or religiously. Did they enable people to better themselves? Did they make the world a better place in which to live? Did they help people reach the goal of liberation, equanimity, peace, Nirvana? And they believed that they did not. They returned to some of the early sayings of the Buddha where he is reported to have criticized an undue preoccupation with philosophical questions as a diversion from the spiritual path. Or, according to the *Heart Sutra,* because the *bodhisattva* relies on "Perfect Wisdom" rather than a rational or quantifiable knowledge, his mind is totally freed from all obstructions and limitations. That is to say, true wisdom, the wisdom gone beyond, does not rely on either objects of sense or concepts based on these objects.

The notion of emptiness as used by the writer of the *Heart Sutra* has a critical function. This critical point of view says basically that nothing can adequately define or symbolize Absolute Truth. Such a perspective has a long history within Buddhism, probably going back to the Buddha himself. In some schools it emerges more forcefully than in others, however. In India in the second century A.D., a philosopher named Nagarjuna formulated this viewpoint in a more logical manner than anyone before him. His teaching attracted other important thinkers, and from this group emerged the Madhyamika (Middle Way) school of Mahayana Buddhist thought. Taking the Dependent Co-origination teaching as a symbol for the relative and conditioned nature of things in the world, Nagarjuna said, therefore, "nothing can

48

come into being, nor can anything cease to exist; nothing is eternal nor does anything have an end; nothing is identical, nor is anything differentiated; nothing moves by itself, nor is it moved by anything else." While this logic is difficult to understand, Nagarjuna's intention is clear. He wanted to destroy reliance on all views or philosophies so that a direct intuition of the highest or spiritual truth could break through. Precisely because the world is conditioned and relative, a system of philosophy that defines the truth completely cannot be devised. The truth is to be found in the dynamic nature of the world, not in its superficial and obvious aspect, but in its hidden and profound aspect. Nagarjuna's command is, "Always go deeper. The secret of life is right in front of you but you have to make a special effort to find the key."

The Zen (Chinese: Ch'an) school of Mahayana Buddhism developed this critical perspective in a unique manner. As discussed in Part I, Zen developed in China and therefore cannot be interpreted simply as an extension of the Indian Wisdom Sutras or the philosophy of Nagarjuna even though they have much in common. Zen developed various methods designed to put students in a mental double-bind situation where they would be forced to think about life in an unconventional manner. There are stories of Zen masters who pushed their disciples off the temple porch into a mud puddle or punched them in the nose as part of the program to jolt them out of their usual, logical way of thinking and thereby to open their minds to a more profound, spiritual insight. Hakuin Zenji, the great eighteenth-century Japanese Zen reformer, was enlightened when he was hit over the head with a broom by an irate housewife while he was deep in thought. Perhaps you have had an analogous experience—a time when you were lost in your own self-reflection and then something totally unrelated occurred, startling you into a profound and unexpected insight. Zen religious training employs such methods. In addition to sometimes using peculiar physical methods (known as "skillful means"), one Zen tradition is particularly famous for its verbal mind twisters (called *koans* in Japanese or *kung'an* in Chinese). Further discussion of *koans* appears in Part III, in connection with the place of meditation in Buddhist practice.

The Mahayana teaching that the truth is not separate from, but is found within, the dynamic world of change and relativity represents the general tendency of this tradition to transform early Buddhism into a religion of universal salvation. The early Mahayana schools saw the Theravadins as overly monastic and exclusivistic, their salvation as too far removed from the present, and their religious practice as too narrow for most people. As Buddhism became more popular in India, it inevitably became less monastic in its orientation and developed conceptions of salvation that were more universal and religious practices that were more readily available to ordinary lay people. This broad distinction between the early Mahayana and Theravada schools is, of course, not entirely fair. As will be seen in Part III, the Theravada tradition developed popular forms as well. However, especially in the area of doctrine, religious teaching and practice, the Mahayana schools were the most liberal and adaptive. The following section examines the Mahayana claim of universal salvation in terms of its teaching about the Buddha, the saint (*bodhisattva,* or wisdom-being), and the universal Buddha nature.

Buddha, Bodhisattva, Buddha Nature

Within the Theravada tradition the Buddha appears as an extraordinary human being who discovered the way to truth and freedom and embodied this way in his *dharma,* or teaching. This conception is reflected in the formula most often used to characterize the Buddha in the Theravada scriptures: "The Blessed One is an *arahat,* a fully awakened one endowed with knowledge and good conduct, happy, a knower of the world, unsurpassed leader able to tame men, teacher of men and gods, the awakened, the blessed." After the Buddha's death, however, two developments took place which radically changed the traditional view of the Buddha as a "teacher of men and gods." The first of these developments was toward abstraction. While the Buddha was alive, he was the living embodiment of his teachings. However, after his death, only his *dharma,* or teaching, remained as the representation of Perfect Truth. The question naturally arose, How could a human being represent such truth? The Mahasanghika (the Great Assembly) school of the late fourth century B.C., one of the forerunners of the Mahayana, developed the notion that the Buddha was a supramundane, transcendental being who was as without blemish as his teaching. However, because he wanted to teach human beings, he only appeared as a man for the purpose of realizing his *dharma,* or truth. This apparitional body was not subject to any imperfections of the flesh. One of the early Wisdom Sutras puts it this way:

> The Blessed One does not derive his name from the fact that he has acquired this physical personality, but from the fact that he has acquired all-knowledge. And this all-knowledge of the Blessed One has come forth from the perfection of wisdom. The physical personality of the Blessed One, on the other hand, is the result of

the skill in means of the perfection of wisdom. And that becomes a sure foundation for the realization of perfect knowledge by others.[13]

A similar controversy arose in the Christian tradition regarding the physical nature of Jesus Christ. One group of early Christians, the Docetists, argued that since God could not assume the imperfections of humanity, Jesus must be a mere apparition or appearance. In the Mahayana school this tendency toward abstraction resulted in the concept of the universal Buddha-body which appeared in various forms on earth and in the heavens. The classical formulation of this notion of the Buddha-body was tripartite. At its highest level (the level of *dharma*) the Buddha-body is without distinction, universal and omnipresent; at the middle level it appears in sublime forms in the Buddha worlds and heavens which form part of the Buddhist cosmology; at the third level are found the Sakyamuni Buddha and other Buddhas who have become incarnate in human history. Such a formulation enabled the Mahayanists to account for the various Buddha forms which emerged in that tradition. Also it enabled them to harmonize both the tendency toward abstraction in their teaching about the Buddha and the tendency to make the Buddha into a deity. This later tendency was very important in the development of the Mahayana as a religion of universal salvation and influenced their teachings about the Buddha and the Mahayana saint-saviors known as *bodhisattvas,* or wisdom-beings.

Some students of religion have claimed that human beings have a natural inclination to worship—to make gods as objects of worship. Buddhism may be a good case in point. In early Buddhist texts the Buddha is quoted as saying that he cannot help anyone attain Nirvana but can only point the way through his teaching. The Buddha, therefore, was not to be worshipped as a savior of any kind. He commanded everyone to work out his own salvation by himself. No savior could be instrumental in that important process of highest self-development and self-fulfillment. Yet before much time had passed, the Buddha began to be worshipped. The human tendency to deify began to have its effect.

One of the first signs of this development was the early importance of Buddha relics. A cult of Buddha relics began at least as early as the time of King Asoka (third century B.C.). Some of the earliest archaeological sites in India are the great Buddhist reliquary mounds *(cetiyas)* at Sanchi and Barhut. Worshippers came to these pilgrimage centers not only to pay respects to the remains of the Buddha but also to gain good fortune through the power the relics were thought to contain. Another sign of the development of the cult of the Buddha as a deity was the construction of Buddha images which began around the first century A.D. The earliest Buddhist archaeological remains at places like Sanchi and Barhut contain bas-reliefs where the Buddha is depicted only by a symbol, for example, a throne or the wheel of the law *(dharma)*. Later, partially through Greek and Persian influences in northwestern India, Buddha images began to be made for the purpose of worship as well as for artistic reasons. At some of the ancient Buddhist sites in Sri Lanka, Buddha images were placed on altars constructed beside the *cetiyas*. Gradually Buddhist worship evolved from mere pilgrimage to making offerings at Buddha altars and finally to a congregational type of worship. Changing concepts of the Buddha accompanied these changing patterns of worship.

The Mahayana tradition developed a full pantheon of Buddhas eventually arranged or structured around a cosmic pattern with principal Buddhas placed at the four cardinal directions. In northern India these cosmic Buddhas were associated with female consorts who personified or symbolized the deity's special powers. The development of male Buddhas and female consorts played an important role in the Buddhist tradition known as the Vajrayana (Thunderbolt Vehicle), also known as the Tantrayana or the Tantric tradition, which came to dominate northern India and Tibet by the seventh century A.D. In Vajrayana teaching and ritual practice, the duality of male and female, interpreted as wisdom and compassion, respectively, plays a very important role. The highest goal of this tradition is even described as the union of compassion and wisdom. Carl Jung, the noted Swiss psychiatrist, had a particular interest in this form of Buddhism. He saw parallels between the Vajrayana view of the world and his understanding of the male and female sides of the human psyche, and he wrote a commentary on one of the famous Tibetan Buddhist texts, *The Tibetan Book of the Dead*. As the latest form of Buddhism to develop in India, the Vajrayana philosophy represents a synthesis of Buddhist thought, and its popular ideas and practices partook of the popular religious culture common to northern India and Central Asia.

Of the several Buddhas that became objects of faith, worship, and cultic devotion, none is more famous than the Buddha Amitabha (known in Japan as the Amida Buddha), the Buddha of infinite light and life. Within the cosmic scheme of Mahayana Buddhism, the Amitabha Buddha is located in the West and, hence, is also known as the Buddha of the Western Paradise, or the Pure Land. Amitabha is celebrated as a savior in three Indian Mahayana sutras, and the glories of the heavenly paradise over which he rules are spelled out in detail. In the *Larger Pure Land Sutra* it is stated that Amitabha's saving power rests in the vast reservoir of merit he has accumulated through countless lifetimes. Hence, those who call upon him in absolute faith can avail themselves of some of this merit. In contrast to the strict doctrine of the Theravadins who insisted that the individual could be saved only through his own merit, the Mahayana tradition based its concept of the Buddha as a savior on a broadened view of karmic merit. This notion has parallels with the Roman Catholic teaching of the merit of the saints as well as the general Christian teaching of salvation through faith.

The transformation of the Buddha from a teacher to a savior had the effect of popularizing Buddhism. It is easy to see how a religion of faith in the miraculous power and good works of a savior-Buddha would have popular appeal. The final goal in this tradition is not postponed for aeons of lifetimes of preparation; it is here now, available through the merit of the Amitabha Buddha. Furthermore, the goal which it promises to the believer is not a vague concept like Nirvana, but a heavenly paradise described in the most extraordinary terms.

> This world, Sukhavati, which is the world system of the Lord Amitabha, is rich and prosperous, comfortable, fertile, delightful and crowded with many Gods and men. And in this world system, there are no hells, no animals, no ghosts. . . .
>
> This world system emits many fragrant odors, it is rich in a great variety of flowers and fruits, adorned with jewel trees, which are frequented by flocks of various birds with sweet voices. . . . Such jewel trees, and clusters of banana trees and rows of palm trees, all made of precious things, grow everywhere in this Buddha-field.[14]

While such a paradise has symbolic meaning for the educated, the common villager believes in its literal reality. Such a mythic description of the Western Paradise is not unlike medieval Christian descriptions of heaven which held the popular imagination of their time.

The Goal

In the Mahayana tradition, salvation is not a far-distant Nirvana realizable only through one's own unstinting efforts in numerous lifetimes. It becomes readily available through the saving power of various Buddhas and their helpers, or savior-saints *(bodhisattvas)*. *Bodhisattvas* have achieved a perfect synthesis of the two principal Buddha virtues, wisdom and compassion, as the *Heart Sutra* pointed out. The term *bodhisattva* has two primary references in the

Mahayana tradition—one on the level of monastic practice and the other in terms of faith and devotion. On the first level, the Mahayana monk takes *bodhisattva* vows. He promises to postpone his own Nirvana until all sentient beings are saved. Thus even though he becomes an enlightened being (a Buddha), he pledges to remain in this realm of *samsara* (rebirth) until everyone else has gained enlightenment. On the second level, the *bodhisattva* is a savior figure in much the same way as the Buddha Amitabha. The most well known of all these saviors is the *bodhisattva* Avalokitesvara, who is associated with the Buddha Amitabha in the Western Paradise. He also is celebrated in numerous Mahayana texts:

> Strong in fine knowledge, Avalokitesvara surveys
> Beings afflicted by countless ills,
> And by many ills oppressed.
> He thus becomes the Savior of the world with its Gods.
>
> Your luster is spotless and immaculate,
> Your knowledge without darkness, your splendor like the sun,
> Radiant like the blaze of a fire not disturbed by the wind,
> Warming the world you shine splendidly.
>
> Eminent in your pity, friendly in your words,
> One great mass of fine virtues and friendly thoughts . . .
> You rain down the rain of the deathless Dharma.[15]

Up to this point this discussion has shown how the Mahayana tradition challenged the exclusivistic tendency of the Theravada tradition philosophically and also how it moved in the direction of a religion of universal salvation through changes in the concept of the Buddha and of Nirvana. In closing, one further comment must be made in regard to the concept of universal Buddhahood. Not only did the Mahayana develop the concept of the Buddha, *bodhisattvas,* and female consorts (e.g., the goddess Tara who is of prominent impor-

This rock garden (top) and Zen temple (bottom)
are two facets of Buddhism in Japan.

tance in Central Asia) as saviors, it also affirmed that all sentient beings are potential Buddhas. It was noted earlier that the Mahayana brought Nirvana into the mundane world or the realm of change and relativity *(samsara)*, making it available to all. The Buddha for Mahayanists is not separated from suffering mankind; all have the Buddha nature within. One simply has to realize that it is there. Shinran Shonen, the founder of the True Pure Land school of Buddhism in the thirteenth century in Japan, represents one consequence of the Mahayana teaching of the universal Buddha nature. He said that one utterance of the name of the Amida Buddha in true faith is sufficient for salvation.

Selected aspects of the vast panorama of Buddhist thought have been covered in Part II. Much has been left unsaid, but it is hoped that a sufficient interest is aroused so that you may use some of the books listed in the Bibliography for further study. Buddhist teachings vary greatly, as this part points out. While there is a common core to the Buddhist world view, in some respects there are as many similarities between devotional theism of the Mahayana Amitabha/Pure Land tradition and Christianity as between this Mahayana tradition and the seemingly austere and simple monastic faith of early Buddhism. Of course, the symbols of Mahayana devotionalism are Buddhist; there is no Amitabha Buddha in Christianity. However, looking beyond the strangeness of the symbols to the meaning behind them reveals more similarities between Buddhism and religions practiced in the West than might be expected. Indeed, part of the challenge of studying Buddhism is to understand not only its uniqueness but also its similarities with other religious traditions, including those of the Western world.

The Practice of Buddhism

Religion is much more than a set of teachings or a system of doctrine. What would a religion be without institutions, rituals, worship, festivals, and moral codes? A religion contains all of these elements, and Buddhism is no exception. Part III, then, will examine those aspects of this tradition having to do with Buddhist practice. In particular, Buddhist rituals, forms of meditation, and ethics, or ways in which Buddhism affects social and political behavior, will be examined. These practices have evolved through several centuries, yet some of them remain relatively unchanged. Others represent the response of Buddhism to modern currents and trends. Similarly, practices in Christianity and Judaism reflect both past traditions as well as contemporary innovations. In the study of religion, it must be kept in mind that a religion is a living organism which remains relevant by adapting to various changes in society. This study of Buddhist practice will attempt to represent both past and contemporary forms. As will be seen, the present does not always rest easily with the past. Young monks demanding changes in religious and political institutions illustrate this point. This study of Buddhist practices will produce other examples of the tensions between past and present. Remember, Buddhism is not an archaic or outdated religion but part of a living history in Asia and throughout the world.

BUDDHIST RITUAL

Ritual practices form a part of every religious tradition. Rituals celebrate the worship of a god, life crises such as death, important events such as joining a church or synagogue, changes in the cycles or seasons of nature, and the history of a religious community. Rituals take many forms. They may be very simple, like a Quaker meeting in which the ritual (if it may be called that) consists of sitting in silence. At the other extreme might be a Russian or Greek Orthodox Easter service filled with many priests, icons, burning incense, and a symbolic reenactment of the resurrection of Jesus.

Religious rituals also occur at many different times. Some may follow an annual calendar. For example, in Christianity Christmas and Easter are celebrated annually as is Rosh Hashanah in Judaism. In these two traditions the ritual Sunday or Sabbath service occurs weekly. And in monasteries daily worship is stipulated in the morning, afternoon, and evening. Rituals stand out as visible reenactments of the beliefs of a religious community, be it Judaism, Christianity, Islam, Hinduism, or Buddhism. Consequently, the study of religious rituals aids the understanding of the teachings or doctrine of a religion, especially those foreign to the student.

In Judaism and Christianity many important rituals center either upon events in the life of the founder (i.e., Moses, Jesus) or upon events occurring in the early years of those communities. Thus Passover commemorates the escape of the Israelites from bondage in Egypt, and Christmas celebrates the birth of Jesus. As might be expected, Buddhist rituals center around events in the Buddha's life and his early community. The principal ritual celebrations in Buddhism commemorate the Buddha's birth, enlightenment, and death (or final Nirvana, as it is called), the occasion when the Buddha is reputed to have preached his first sermon (see Part II), and the time when 1,250 of his disciples miraculously converged at a common meeting place in northern India to listen to the Buddha's exposition of his philosophy. Taken together, these events represent the "Three Gems" of Buddhism: (1) the Buddha, (2) his teaching *(dharma)*, and (3) his community of monks *(sangha)*.

Buddhists consider Visakha Puja *(puja,* or worship, which occurs during the lunar month of Visakha) to be the most important ritual celebration. They believe that the Buddha's birth, enlightenment, and death occurred miraculously on the same day—a demonstration of the Buddha's power and superhuman qualities extending over time itself.

In Theravada Buddhist countries like Thailand, Visakha Puja, celebrated in May, reflects other beliefs as well, many of them non-Buddhist in nature. For example, because the rainy season begins in May, some elements of this celebration are related to the start of the planting season. And in the particular case described in the following section, Visakha Puja includes the annual celebration of the founding of the temple. At first, it may seem that the Buddha, the beginning of the planting season, and a temple's founding have little in common, yet each represents a new beginning (a religious way, a new agricultural cycle, and a new temple). This combination of Buddhist and non-Buddhist elements is not really surprising since major Jewish and Christian celebrations reflect a similar integration or synthesis.

58

Indeed, the timing of Christmas during the winter solstice and Easter at the beginning of spring has origins in non-Christian elements.

Following this brief discussion of the general features of religious rituals, some specific examples of rituals in the Buddhist tradition in Thailand will be examined: (1) a Visakha Puja celebration at a major temple in northern Thailand, (2) the Buddhist New Year celebration, and (3) Buddhist death rituals. In countries like Thailand, Burma, Cambodia, and Sri Lanka, Buddhist rituals provide signposts which dramatize the beliefs Buddhists hold about the nature of the world. Thus even though Buddhist rituals are bound to life-cycle events (birth and death) and to the cycles or rhythms of nature, they are primarily expressions of Buddhist beliefs and teachings. Similarly in the West, the events of the life cycle—birth, puberty, marriage, death—are sanctified by Jewish and Christian ceremonies.

Visakha Puja

Visakha Puja occurs on the full-moon day of the sixth lunar month. While officially celebrating the major events in the Buddha's life, the ritual also celebrates the onset of the monsoon rains. Thus Visakha Puja signifies the beginning of the Buddhist religion and anticipates the start of another agricultural season, all of which occurs at the midpoint of the lunar calendar. The celebration to be described here takes place at a large temple in the northern Thai town of Lamphun.

It begins (as is true for many Buddhist ceremonies) very early in the morning as crowds of lay people enter the temple grounds to give food to the monks. Because Buddhist monks of the Theravada tradition of Southeast Asia are forbidden by monastic law from receiving money, devout lay people provide them with the necessities of life. In Thailand monks can customarily be seen at sunrise on daily alms rounds, yet on important occasions such as Visakha Puja, food is brought to the temple instead. The act of giving food to the monks has a twofold mutually beneficial result: it frees the monks from undue concern with material things while it reaps spiritual benefits or rewards for the giver. Buddhists believe that providing for the material welfare of the monks earns religious merit to benefit the giver in some future existence. Major celebrations are, then, especially important times in which to earn such merit.

After the food is presented to the monks, a variety of activities take place in and around the temple. Many form part of the temple's anniversary celebration which began several days prior to Visakha Puja. This celebration can be described as a combination of festival, fair, and carnival, with evening carnival-like rides, games of chance, and booths selling snacks and souvenirs. The main morning activity is a hot-air balloon competition. Temples from all over Lamphun enter this festivity with large tissue-paper balloons from which strings of firecrackers are suspended. The air inside each balloon is heated by inserting a bamboo pole with ignited kerosene rags on the end. Inevitably a few of the fragile balloons go up in flames. When each balloon is ready, the fuse to a long string of firecrackers is lit. As their loyal supporters cheer encouragement, the balloons soar high into the sky, fireworks blazing.

What does such a competition have to do with the three focal events in the Buddha's life, those celebrated in Visakha Puja? On one level, religious festivals of which the competition is a part reinforce community solidarity while serving as a major source of community entertainment. The most successful balloons bring a certain amount of honor to the sponsoring temples. Indeed, some would even say that they earn merit for the people who made them. On another level, the balloons soaring into the sky with the accompanying firecrackers might be interpreted as a relic of a more primitive rain-making ceremony. Yet another interpretation finds some Buddhists believing that the balloons are conveying offerings to one of the Buddhist heavens where Buddha relics are enshrined. In return for such offerings it is hoped that the ruling deity of this heaven will shower blessings upon the people participating in this event. In spite of these interpretations, the fact remains that the balloon competition is just plain fun, especially for the young people who make and launch them.

Following the balloon competition one can eat a quick lunch of barbeque chicken or pork on a stick, some fruit, and tea, all bought from the numerous food stalls and vendors who have set up shop in the temple grounds. Next is the major event of the early afternoon—the long drum competition. The northern Thai long drum is a splendid percussion instrument. The base, consisting of a hollow piece of wood measuring up to ten feet in length and mounted on wheels, provides a profound and haunting sound. Traditionally the long drum was struck at regular intervals on the evening prior to the Buddhist sabbath, its deep tones reverberating across the countryside. Now only a few temples continue to observe this custom. Today Buddhists from many temples in the surrounding area have brought their long drums into the temple compound to see which one will be judged to have the best tone and be beaten the most skillfully. The first drum is struck very rapidly until the drummer's arm is exhausted. A piece of cloth is wound around his hand making a cone-shaped "beater," yet even so, the pressure exerted during the drumming can break a wrist or a hand. Others take their turn until all have played and a winner is declared. How can the long drum event be interpreted as part of a Visakha Puja celebration? The entertainment value cannot be denied, but once again a Buddhist meaning is sought. One of them goes as follows:

> Once upon a time a demon decided that mankind should be destroyed because all the people in the world were so evil. The God, Indra, hearing of the demon's intention, pleaded with him to have mercy. Indra seemed to be getting nowhere with his arguments until, in the midst of his pleading, the sound of a long drum was heard announcing the Buddhist sabbath. Indra then succeeded in convincing the demon that the drum sound proved that the people were still devoted to the Buddha and were, therefore, not evil.

So it is believed that Indra saves or rewards those who perform meritorious deeds, in this case, the beating of the long drum.

After these fun-filled preliminaries, the most important of the day's celebrations begins around the large pinnacled dome, or *cetiya,* of the temple, thought to contain relics of the Buddha. Veneration of relics plays an important role in popular Buddhism. Pilgrimage to places where Buddha relics are thought to be enshrined has been and continues to be a frequently performed act of devotion and piety. This particular temple in Lamphun has a beautiful gold-leafed covered *cetiya.* Lay people honor it by pouring or throwing holy water on its base and sides. Such an act amounts to a ritual cleansing and undoubtedly is part of a ritualistic enactment of the beginning of a new Buddhist year.

As evening approaches another event occurs near the *cetiya.* Around dusk crowds of lay people follow the monks and novices from the temple in a clockwise circling of the *cetiya* three times. They hold lighted candles and incense in their hands as they wend their way slowly around this sacred spot, clouds of fragrant smoke filling the air. On each of the three rounds, they reflect on the virtues of the Buddha, his teaching, and the monastic order. Having completed this act of veneration, the congregation enters the main temple to listen to a long sermon which recounts the major events in the Buddha's life beginning with the wedding of the Buddha's parents and ending with the decline of Buddhism in India. This long sermon lasts nearly the entire night with several monks preaching. Many of the congregation sleep through part of the sermon; yet even so, after such a busy day the night provides a test of patience and endurance.

Thus the Visakha Puja celebration combines different elements—entertainment, the beginning of the agricultural year, and, most importantly, a commemoration or ritual reenactment of the Buddha's life and ministry.

The Buddhist New Year Celebration

Another Buddhist ritual centers on the Thai New Year. April signals the end of the dry season and the beginning of the monsoon rains, thus giving it an important agricultural significance. Many of the New Year ritual elements appear to be magical attempts to entice the rains necessary for rice cultivation. The New Year ceremony also reflects Hindu or Brahmanic meanings in addition to Buddhist ones, as the following story of its origin indicates.

> Once there was a wealthy, childless couple. Their home was near the dwelling of a drunken n'er-do-well who had two children with golden colored skin. One day the n'er-do-well in a drunken rage berated his wealthy neighbors by shouting that the most shameful thing for someone with wealth was having no children to inherit that wealth. The couple felt very sad and prayed to the gods for three years that they might have a child. Finally, at the time when the sun leaves the sign of Pisces in the zodiac and enters that of Aries (usually around April 13), they took an offering of rice and after washing it seven times presented it to a large banyan tree growing on the river bank and prayed for a son. The tree deity was moved by their plight and

A cetiya containing relics of the Buddha. A cetiya has three parts: a base, a rounded dome, and a pointed top.

devotion and pleaded their cause to the god Indra that they be given a son. Indra granted their wish, and the boy was named Dhammapala. For him was built a seven-storied palace near the banyan tree. He was especially clever, learning the language of the birds, memorizing the sacred texts by the time he was seven, and becoming adept in fortune-telling.

At that time everyone in the world worshipped the Lord Kapilabrahma who had the power to determine the fortune of men. When Kapilabrahma heard about Dhammapala, he went to see him and proposed a wager: he would ask three questions and if Dhammapala was unable to answer within seven days he would be beheaded; but, if he answered them correctly, the same fate would befall Kapilabrahma. The three questions were: Where is the zodiac in the morning, in the afternoon, and in the evening?

Six days passed and Dhammapala still had not discovered the answer. Knowing he would be killed the next day according to the terms of the wager, he decided it would be better to hide and simply starve to death. So he descended from his palace and found his way to two palm trees beneath which he fell asleep. Two eagles were in the palm trees, and at dusk the female asked her mate what they would eat the next day. Her mate replied that they would feast upon Dhammapala who would be killed by Kapilabrahma since he was unable to answer the questions. The female asked what were the questions, and when her mate replied, she asked what the answers were. He said, "In the morning the zodiac is at our face so we wash it; in the afternoon it is at our breast so we sprinkle the breast with scented water; in the evening it is at our feet so we wash our feet."

Dhammapala, overhearing this conversation, returned to the palace. The next day when Kapilabrahma came the boy was able to answer the questions. Kapilabrahma then sent for the seven servants of the god Indra. "I must cut off my head as an offering for Dhammapala," he said. "However, if my head is put into the earth, the earth will be consumed by fire. If it is cast into the air, there will be no more rain. If it is put into the ocean, it will be dried up. Therefore, let these seven servants of Indra take my head around Mount Sumeru (the largest and central mountain in Indian cosmology) within sixty minutes' time and then put it in the cave in the mountain made out of seven precious stones. Indra's servants should then make offerings for 365 days which constitute one year. Then at this same time every year Indra's servants should take my head around Mount Sumeru again."

This richly symbolic story tells in mythic fashion how the traditional Thai New Year began. The next part of this discussion reveals how the story is woven into the celebration itself.

The New Year celebration takes place over several days. The first day signifies the end of the old year. On this day houses are thoroughly cleaned, trash burned, clothes washed. From midnight until dawn the sound of exploding firecrackers can be heard. In this manner all the evils of the past year are banished. The second day serves as a preparation for the following day, an interim before the beginning of the New Year itself. Special foods are prepared to be taken to the temple the next morning as food offerings for the monks. In the late afternoon sand is brought to the temple from a nearby river and then fashioned into a large pyramidal *cetiya*. Each lay person brings as much sand as can be carried, and it is added to the already growing pile and decorated with flags on top. All is in readiness for the third day, the most important and auspicious, for it signifies the beginning of the New Year. Arising early in the morning, the lay people bring food offerings to the monks. They wait for the dedication of the sand pyramid, marking the true beginning of the New Year. The *cetiya* can be interpreted as a miniature Mount Sumeru, and the offerings, as the ones Indra's servants were to make in order to avert both fire and drought and to ensure rain for the planting season. Once the sand pyramid is dedicated, the sand is spread around the temple compound to provide a new and higher ground level before the beginning of the monsoon rains.

Customs during the remaining third and fourth days differ from town to town and from temple to temple. Some lay people visit the temple to pay their respects to the venerable monks and to the Buddha image, bathing it with scented water. Others purchase fish or small caged birds to set free. Freeing fish and birds is considered a meritorious act, which reflects the Buddhist attitude of respect for all living creatures. Paying respects to venerable monks as well as family elders emphasizes the fact that at the beginning of the New Year social relationships would be reestablished to ensure harmony in the community. Indeed, in former times some creditors would release debtors of their debts, a practice generally not followed today.

One other New Year custom should be mentioned—the throwing of water on unwary passersby. Young people in particular delight in this custom and it sometimes gets out of hand, especially in larger towns.

At a deeper level, a blessing of water poured over the hands of one's elders, parents, or teachers is an act of respect just as is the pouring of scented holy water over the Buddha images. In the story related earlier, the answers to the questions put to Dhammapala involved the use of water. At this particular dry, hot, dusty time of year, water is precious and scarce. Perhaps in earlier times the gods were enticed to send forth rain through such water-blessing acts. The custom of playful, often rowdy water throwing, not tolerated at other times, also signifies the end of the old year and the beginning of the new. With their exuberance spent, the celebrators enter the New Year with a clean slate!

Thus in this way is Thai New Year celebrated. The old year is ushered out, the new agricultural year soon begins, community solidarity is affirmed, and opportunities for making religious merit as well as for having fun are provided. While Buddhist monks participate in temple-related ceremonies, the New Year celebration is not as religiously significant to the Buddhist community as is Visakha Puja.

Buddhist Death Rituals

The third type of ritual occasion to be considered concerns death or end-of-life-cycle rituals. Buddhism throughout Asia has been most consistently connected with death rituals. In China and Japan where Confucianism and Taoism have competed with Buddhism (see *Religion in China* in this series), funerals and death anniversary celebrations are particularly associated with Buddhist temples. Even in Zen Buddhism, ordinarily thought of as a contemplative or meditative tradition, funerals and death anniversary rituals are among the most important activities of the temple priest. And in the Theravada countries of Southeast Asia, funerals are more closely associated with Buddhism than are birth ceremonies or weddings. Why is this the case? Some with a Western bias have pointed to Buddhism's

A funeral carriage for an abbot, in the shape of a mythological bird. Note the picture of the deceased in the foreground, beside the altar.

pessimistic attitude toward the world. However, observation of a Buddhist funeral service reveals a deeper interpretation.

All religions provide death rituals. These ease the loss of the deceased for the survivors, serve to reinforce the teachings of that particular religion regarding death and the afterlife, and often bring together family members who live apart. Buddhist funerals contain all these elements. In China and Japan they serve to propitiate the spirits of the deceased so that they will be happy and will not punish those relatives still living. In Southeast Asian Buddhist countries, the funeral is an opportunity to honor the deceased as well as to gain spiritual merit for the living and the dead.

Inside the funeral hall, a building adjacent to the temple, the family is seated at the front with the monks filing in to take their places on a raised platform to one side. At the front of the room lies the casket surrounded with flowers and gifts the family will present to the monks. After everyone is assembled, the monks chant portions of Buddhist scripture followed by a sermon instructing those present in the Buddhist belief in rebirth. Afterward food and other gifts are presented to the monks. Such gift giving is believed to be spiritually beneficial both for the deceased and the givers. The hope is that both will have a happier and more prosperous existence in the next life. The orientation is not pessimistic, as some say; rather the emphasis is upon life—the next life after death. For this reason a Buddhist funeral in Thailand seems more like a festival than a funeral. In one area people are busily preparing rice and curries for the monks while festive music is played on traditional instruments. Old friends greet each other, and children play games in the sand. Crying or other signs of grief are seldom shown—unless, of course, the death is particularly untimely or tragic.

Buddhist rituals vary greatly in form and meaning depending upon the particular cultural context in which they flourish. For example, Buddhist rituals tend to be very elaborate in Tibet and Nepal. Temples are colorfully painted and decorated, monks may be ornately costumed, and rituals may include elaborate hand gestures and a multiscaled, styled chant. At the other extreme, Zen Buddhist temples are architecturally austere, colored only by the natural woods and straw matting. Zen priests wear black, plainly designed robes and chant in a less elaborate style than their Tibetan or Nepalese counterparts. These few examples give an idea of how richly varied Buddhist rituals are. As more is learned about Buddhist practices, ceremonies may seem less foreign to our Western ways of religious practice.

BUDDHIST MEDITATION

The term *meditation* once was a strange, little understood word. Today, however, many people, young and old alike, are practicing forms of meditation. Transcendental Meditation is one of the more popular forms being used by Americans. Some public school systems have even adopted a brief period of meditation as part of the daily routine. Meditation techniques are used more and more by psychologists and psychiatrists in therapy, and greater emphasis is being placed on meditation in some Christian circles. So the mystique that formerly surrounded meditation is gradually wearing off as more Americans are exposed to it. Still questions remain: Did meditation originate with Buddhism? Is Buddhist meditation unique?

Meditation is said to be the single most important religious practice in Buddhism. Buddhist texts reveal that the practice of meditation or mental training played an important role in the Buddhist monastic community in India where Buddhism was founded. Later, as Buddhism became a popular religion for the masses, proportionately fewer monks actually devoted much of their time to meditation. Temple and ritual activities diverted their attention from the pursuit of wisdom and equanimity produced by the practice of meditation. In short, mental training, concentration exercises, and meditation—those monastic disciplines aimed at the realization of Nirvana—became more and more exceptional.

Today in the Theravada Buddhist countries of Southeast Asia, monks usually pursue meditation only in special monasteries or remote hermitages. And in the Mahayana traditions of East Asia (China, Japan, Korea), principally only Ch'an or Zen Buddhism is noted for its emphasis upon rigorous meditative training. In some Buddhist countries, most notably Burma, there has been a revival of meditation in the past two or three decades. Meditation centers for both monks and laity are often filled with dozens of meditators, especially on weekends. Yet despite this revival, the serious pursuit of the goals of meditation—namely wisdom and equanimity—is the exception rather than the rule. Nevertheless, almost all Buddhists would agree that it is through the practice of meditation rather than the performance of religious rituals that Nirvana is attained.

Buddhists can hardly be criticized for not taking meditation more seriously. Not all Christians or Jews faithfully practice the more rigorous disciplines of their traditions. Even those who consider themselves "religious" without formal membership in a church or synagogue exert little effort in religious practices. In every religious tradition there is a disparity between the ideal and the way it is practiced. The object in this book is not to make such value judgments. Rather it is to learn as much as possible about Buddhism, its goals, and the people who pursue those goals. Such knowledge will serve to enrich our experience, produce a tolerance for differences, and cause us to reflect upon our own religious background. By sympathetically entering into another's way of life, hopefully we can begin to understand our own better.

What is the nature of Buddhist meditation? Is it the same as TM, Yoga, or other forms of mental training associated with Asian religions? Some similarities can be found among many of these forms of discipline. For example, nearly all of them describe meditation as producing a sense of calm, and recently different forms of meditation have been shown scientifically to produce similar physiological effects, such as lowering breathing and metabolic rates and changing brain-wave patterns. Yet there are decided differences among meditation disciplines. Yoga may utilize a variety of physical postures. Transcendental Meditation offers an easily learned technique for quieting the mind, especially suited to the harried American life-style. Forms of meditative practice vary widely even within Buddhism itself; however, this discussion focuses on the basic teachings of Buddhist Insight Meditation, much of which applies to other forms of mental training. (For further study, see suggested titles in the Bibliography.)

Awareness or mindfulness is the basic principle of Insight Meditation. The Buddha taught the necessity of overcoming one's basic misunderstanding about oneself and the world. To cut through the illusion, to dispel the mirage, to see things as they really are demands constant attention. In the broadest sense, Insight Meditation is nothing more or less than constant attentiveness. The Buddha rightly assumed that most people look at the world and see what they *want* to see rather than what is *really* there. To break the habit of looking but not seeing, of hearing but not listening, requires a special effort. Think of the times today, last week, or last month that you acted on the basis of inadequate or inaccurate information; or, even more to the point,

A monk practicing meditation.

think about how many actions, gestures, and thoughts within the last hour were largely unconsciously and thoughtlessly motivated. An honest look reveals the truth of the Buddha's teaching—a state of mindlessness, a lack of awareness.

How can such habits be broken? How can a state of total awareness or mindfulness be achieved? In the Buddhist view such an achievement does not come easily. One's usual business cannot be pursued in the same old way. Ordinary routines all too often reinforce uninformed and habitual patterns of perception, thought, and action. Like the athlete who works hard to get his body into shape for a track meet, the Buddha teaches the necessity of training the mind in order to overcome these habitual ways of distorting reality.

One of the best-known programs of Buddhist Insight Meditation is found in the text *Foundation of Mindfulness*. It offers a systematic approach for developing awareness based on selective consciousness. Selective consciousness attempts to restrain the sensory inputs to the mind. Try this for a moment. Instead of taking notice of the various tactile, audio, and visual stimuli that usually bombard you, try to shut out as many extraneous sensations, perceptions, and thoughts as you can so that you can be aware of *one thing at a time*. Hard, isn't it? Too many noises outside the room? Thoughts keep creeping in? Uncomfortable from too much lunch or a hard chair?

In order to make it easier, Insight Meditation begins by establishing a condition of relative sensory deprivation—fancy words for saying that the meditator finds a quiet place, settles into a firm sitting posture (traditionally the lotus posture where one sits on the ground or floor with one leg crossed over the other with both feet resting on the thighs), and closes the eyes. The meditator then focuses attention upon *one* object. As in Yoga, Insight Meditation focuses upon the breath. The purpose of focusing on the breath is to try to be aware of only the breath in a fully conscious manner. Breathing for most people is an unconscious act unless, of course, they have a cold or feel short of breath after strenuous exercise. Breathing, then, becomes the first meditation object in the attempt to be fully aware.

Try assuming the condition of relative sensory deprivation yourself. Now seated in a quiet place, your back straight, legs crossed, eyes closed, concentrate on the inhalation and exhalation of your breath, entering and leaving your body. Some breaths are longer than others; the rhythm is hard to maintain. Once you are able to be fully conscious of your breath, then you can graduate to other meditation objects. In the *Foundation of Mindfulness* text, four different kinds of meditation objects are given: (1) those of the body such as the breath, (2) sensations like hot or cold, pleasure or pain, (3) aspects of consciousness such as hatred or lust, which give the mind a particular bias or inclination, and (4) ideas, especially those from the Buddha's teachings—for example, the doctrine of the not-self. In this manner, a mental journey takes the meditator from awareness of the body (breath in this case) to the mind itself, then finally to ideas, discarding along the way attachment to body, feelings, and ideas.

Insight Meditation literally means "sight within," seeing or confronting in a disciplined way life processes (breathing, sensory stimuli, emotions, ideas) as they actually occur. No magic is used, no outside stimuli are employed, no hallucinogenic drugs are taken. Mindfulness minimizes or eliminates ego hang-ups and illusions which so often rule a person. The meditator gains control over his or her life by being able to discriminate between the illusory and the "really real." For the dedicated practitioner the rewards of meditation are great. Yet, one does not meditate to *gain* anything. One meditates simply to be able to *see* things as they really are in order to be as one really is. Self-understanding and self-acceptance, then, are the rewards.

A different form of mental training, developed within one of the Zen traditions, uses seemingly eccentric and paradoxical methods. For example, the meditator might be given a nonrational, logically unanswerable question, called a *koan,* such as "What is the sound of one hand clapping?" After pondering the problem, the student would approach his teacher with a solution. The teacher's responses to the honest efforts of the student would seem bizarre to a Westerner. He might totally ignore the student, hit him with a stick, or shove him off the temple porch into a mud puddle. Such unusual methods of provoking a solution to a rationally unsolvable problem force the student to persevere until he *sees* the answer to the riddle, that is, until he becomes enlightened. The point that the Zen master is forcing his student to make is this: realization of spiritual truth is different from solving an intellectual problem. Realizing such truth demands a radically different mode of thinking and a change in being. In the Buddhist sense, to grasp Nirvana demands a moral transformation. It means changing from being basically ego- or self-centered to being so open and free that one could be called a "not-self." This discovery comes about through the discipline of meditation.

Another method of meditation within the Mahayana traditions uses a *mantra,* a word or phrase used to focus attention. Perhaps the two best-known Japanese Buddhist *mantras* are (1) *Namo Amida Butsu,* "Homage to the Amida Buddha" (the Buddha thought by Japanese

Buddhists of the Pure Land school to preside over the Pure Land or the Western Paradise) and (2) *Nam Myoho Renge Kyo,* "Homage to the Lotus Sutra." The second *mantra* celebrates one of the most important scriptures in the Japanese tradition. These phrases may be repeated over and over again, or they may become only objects of mental concentration while the worshipper manipulates rosarylike beads. Similar practices can be seen in the Christian tradition: the saying of the Hail Mary while counting the rosary and the Greek Orthodox monastic tradition of the constant repetition of the Jesus prayer. Such repetition of a prayer or *mantra* can have a hypnotic or trancelike effect, yet that is not the goal. In Buddhist meditation self-hypnosis is never an end in itself, although it may be a by-product of serious, intensive meditation. Buddhist texts recognize that such trance states are potentially dangerous and that for this reason, intensive meditation should be done only under the expert guidance of a qualified and accomplished meditation teacher.

What about the numerous meditation groups that are developing in the United States? What is their connection to Buddhism? Some of them, like Transcendental Meditation, have no connection at all. Others, such as the Rochester and San Francisco Zen centers, do. In general, Buddhist meditation centers in the United States follow three traditions: Japanese Zen Buddhism, Tibetan Buddhism, and Southeast Asian Theravada Buddhism. Most of the centers have able, experienced teachers who have been trained in Japan, India, Burma, or Sri Lanka. Almost all of them make arrangements for nonresidents to learn meditation techniques at their centers. A partial list of the Buddhist meditation centers in America is included in the Appendix.

BUDDHIST ETHICS

Some Western scholars writing about Buddhism picture it as world rejecting. They say that the goal of Nirvana is otherworldly and that meditation, the method of realizing this goal, is impractical as a way of living in the world. Such an interpretation of Buddhism has an element of truth in it, yet it leaves out a wide variety of other responses Buddhists make. For example, most practicing Buddhists are as concerned to live happily in the world as non-Buddhists, and they, too, have a system of ethics to show the way they are to live in this world. As pointed out in Part II, the Buddhist Eightfold Path stresses the centrality of moral virtue including right action and right vocation. Moral virtue functions as the foundation stone upon which the higher pursuits of meditation and wisdom are built. In his book *Buddhist*

Ethics, the Venerable Saddhatissa, the Sinhalese monk who directs a Buddhist center in London, has observed that the fundamental concern of the Buddha was an ethical one. The Buddha was not interested in constructing a philosophical system. Indeed, as seen in Part II, the Buddha taught that speculation about metaphysical questions such as whether or not the world was eternal or noneternal was useless. Likewise, the Buddha would consider many questions debated by Christian and Jewish theologians a waste of time. In this sense the Buddha's message was a practical or ethical one. For his followers he outlined a way that would eliminate hatred, greed, destructive ambition, and all exploitative activities aimed at self-enhancement at the expense of others. By following this way, a moral and ethical transformation would take place. In countries such as Thailand, primary and secondary students study a required ethics curriculum based primarily on Buddhism.

Ethics, then, form the focus of the Buddha's teaching. Not unlike the law of Moses in Judaism, the Buddha teaches his followers not to kill, not to lie or tell slanderous stories, not to commit acts of fornication, not to steal his neighbor's property, and not to take intoxicants or hallucinogenic drugs. Elsewhere in the texts, the Buddha advises children to respect their parents and parents to be responsible for their children. Buddhist ethics are the formal moral rules faithful Buddhists are to follow much like the Torah was for the Israelites. Rather than detailing these rules in a dry fashion, the abbot in a village temple might instruct Buddhist lay persons by relating the rules in story form. Telling stories illustrated by beautifully painted murals on the temple walls is a more effective and interesting teaching method, especially for those unable to read. Abstract concepts are more difficult to comprehend than are lively stories. People can identify with stories and internalize the moral being taught.

In the Theravada traditions of Southeast Asia some of the best-known stories, called *Jatakas,* relate episodes from the previous lives of the Buddha before his final birth as Siddhartha Gautama. Many of them were originally popular folktales adopted later by Buddhism to illustrate particular virtues. Of the more than five hundred *Jataka* stories in the canonical scriptures of Theravada Buddhism, the last ten are the most beloved. They illustrate the major virtues which, Buddhists believe, are collectively represented by the Buddha himself. Indian legends form the basis for folktales in many Southeast Asian countries. The Indian names for people and places may sound strange to Westerners but not to their listeners who delight in such details. Each story's hero is referred to as a *bodhisattva.* The term literally means "a being filled with wisdom," but in this context it refers to the Buddha in one of his earlier existences or incarnations.

Imagine a Buddhist temple on sabbath day. Lay people enter the dimly lit temple and place flowers and incense before the altar. They wait for the monks to appear. When seated, the monks begin chanting; the faithful laity, seated on the floor, bow their heads and place their hands in an attitude of respectful attentiveness. When the chanting is finished, the abbot begins his sermon by reading from one of the popular *Jataka* stories summarized below.

TEMIYA *(illustrating renunciation)*

Temiya, only son of the king of Benares, overhears his father sentencing four robbers to terrible punishment. Knowing that such action leads to rebirth in hell for 80,000 years and that when he becomes king he must also perform similar actions, Temiya feigns the role of a crippled mute. Understandably disturbed, his parents devise various trials such as withholding food, placing him in a burning hut, having serpents coil around him; yet throughout he remains silent and motionless. Finally, all else failing, the prince is condemned to death and burial. Having been released from his obligation to succeed his father, he reveals his true *bodhisattva* form and assumes the life of an ascetic. His example inspires his parents to become ascetic, thus releasing the king from the punishment of hell.

MAHAJANAKA *(illustrating perseverance)*

Mahajanaka is the son of the king of Mithila who was killed by his brother before Mahajanaka's birth. At her husband's death the queen escapes to the city of Kalacampa with the help of the god Sakka. There a kindly Brahman priest takes her in. When Mahajanaka is sixteen, his mother tells him the story of his father's death, and he resolves to regain the kingdom. He boards a ship for Suvannabhumi and after seven days the ship sinks. Throughout numerous trials and tribulations Mahajanaka perseveres until at last a goddess, the guardian of the sea, helps rescue him. Mahajanaka, being truly a *bodhisattva,* is then chosen as the king of Mithila only to realize that possessions bring nothing but sorrow. He becomes an ascetic eventually to be reborn in heaven.

SAMA *(illustrating loving-kindness)*

Sama is the son miraculously given to Dukulaka and Parika, an ascetic couple living in penance for an evil deed done by their father many lifetimes ago. When Sama is sixteen his parents lose their eyesight, and he faithfully looks after their every need. So gentle is he that even the deer befriend him. One evening while drawing water from a pond, Sama is shot with a poisoned arrow by the king of Benares. The king is filled with sorrow at this accident, and because of his remorse, this evil deed is forgiven by the gods. Through Sama's parents' suffering and grief their penance is ended, and through their cleansing tears Sama is restored to life.

NEMI *(illustrating resolution)*

Nemi is the last king in the Makhadeva line, all of his successors having in old age entered the ascetic life and attained heaven. Nemi becomes renowned for his righteousness and generosity but is not satisfied with himself. He cannot resolve the question: Is it more fruitful to lead a holy life or to be faithful in almsgiving to the poor? Pleased with Nemi's good deeds, the gods send Matali, the charioteer, to bring Nemi to them. On the way he passes through various hells and heavens before reaching the abode of Sakka. After seven days he returns to describe to his people the punishments awaiting evildoers and the rewards for those doing good.

MAHOSODHA *(illustrating wisdom)*

Mahosodha, the fifth and most brilliant sage of King Videha of Mithila, is known for his great wisdom. Many times he is put to the test, always wise enough to solve the riddle. One day two women are brought before him, each claiming to be the mother of the same child. Wise Mahosodha has each of them take the child by a hand and a foot and attempt to pull him over a designated line. When the child cries out in pain, the real mother lets go.

VESSANTARA *(illustrating selfless giving)*

Vessantara, the son of the king of Sivi, incurs the wrath of the populace when he allows eight Brahmans from a neighboring kingdom to take away Sivi's magical white elephant which has rain-making powers. The people force Sanjaya, Vessantara's father, to expel the prince to a far-off forest. Before he goes Vessantara gives away nearly all of his possessions and departs only with his wife, Maddi, his two children, and a chariot drawn by eight horses. Leaving the city, Vessantara is requested to give away his horses and chariot which he does willingly. Proceeding on foot the prince and his family reach their destination deep in the forest. There they live happily for four months until one day an old Brahman, Jujaka, appears and asks Vessantara for his children that they might be servants to his young wife. Vessantara again consents. As a final test of his generosity, the god Indra disguises himself and asks Vessantara to give up Maddi, his wife and last possession. Vessantara again complies and in so doing proves the depth of his self-giving nature. The prince is then rewarded by the gods, receiving back manyfold all he had willingly surrendered.

The Mahayana traditions also teach through stories from the lives of holy and virtuous people. Instead of a legendary ideal, various schools and Buddhist sects in Tibet, China, and Japan look to a particularly wise and devout teacher for their inspiration. Often these schools of thought are characterized more by such important teachers than by doctrinal beliefs. The following stories from the Zen tradition embody virtues held in high esteem by such schools.

Many pupils were studying meditation under the Zen master Sengai. One of them would arise at night, climb over the temple wall, and go to town on a pleasure jaunt. Sengai, inspecting the dormitory quarters, found his pupil missing one night and also discovered the high stool he had used to scale the wall. Sengai removed the stool and stood there in its place. When the wanderer returned, not knowing that Sengai was the stool, he placed his feet on his master's head and jumped down onto the ground. Discovering what he had done, he was most embarrassed. Sengai then said, "It is very chilly in the early morning. Do be careful not to catch cold!" The pupil never went out at night again.

Tanzan and Ekido were once traveling together down a muddy road. A heavy rain was falling. Coming around a bend, they met a lovely girl in a silk kimono and sash who was unable to cross the intersection. "Come on, girl," said Tanzan at once. Lifting her in his arms, he carried her over the mud. Ekido did not speak again until that night when they reached a lodging temple. When he could no longer restrain himself, he said to Tanzan, "We monks don't go near females, especially not young and lovely ones. It is dangerous. Why did you do that?" "I left the girl there," said Tanzan. "Are you still carrying her?"

Nan-in, a Japanese master, received a university professor who came to inquire about Zen. Nan-in served tea. He poured his visitor's cup full, but then kept on pouring. The professor watched the overflow until he could no longer restrain himself. "It is too full. No more will go in!" "Like this cup," Nan-in said, "you are full of your opinions and speculations. How can I show you Zen unless you first empty your cup?"

Up to this point, this discussion of Buddhist ethics has focused on traditional moral virtues and ideal models of those virtues. Do they accurately reflect Buddhism in modern Asia? With what kind of voice is Buddhism speaking to contemporary social, political, and economic problems? What is the future of Buddhism in an increasingly secular, industrialized world? Weighty as these questions are, Buddhism has responded in the area of political change as well as in the social and economic sphere.

As seen in Part I, Buddhism was adopted as a state ideology by the Indian ruler Asoka (third century B.C.), one of the great unifiers of India. Rulers in almost all Asian countries where Buddhism became a major religion found its teachings similarly useful. Indeed, it could be argued that where Buddhism became a popular or broadly based religion, it did so through the support of the ruling classes. Certainly, that was true in Japan, Korea, northern China, Nepal, Tibet, and several Southeast Asian countries.

While Buddhism may have been politically important in the past, what has it contributed to political change and development in the modern period? In countries like Sri Lanka, Burma, and Vietnam, Buddhism was a major factor in the independence movements at the end of the colonial period. From the beginnings of the independence movement in Sri Lanka in the late nineteenth and early twentieth centuries, Buddhism was a key factor. The election of a strongly independent, nationalistic prime minister in 1958 was accomplished with the help of politically active Buddhist monks. A similar pattern occurred in Burma where the independence movement was born in the crucible of strong religious feeling. In Burma and other Theravada countries it is customary to remove one's shoes before entering a temple or other religious precincts considered particularly holy. The British refused to take off their shoes when entering the compound of the Shwedegon Pagoda, one of the holiest spots in Burma. The monks' angry response to this refusal culminated in a protest in 1918, marking the beginning of the anti-British independence movement in Burma. While in both Sri Lanka and Burma the anticolonial/proindependence movements were gradually taken over by secular forces, the initial impetus came either from Buddhist monks or from laymen who considered Buddhism and their national culture to be synonymous.

Vietnam offers a more recent example of the involvement of Buddhism in the affairs of state. Some of you may remember the stories and news photos of Vietnamese Buddhist monks burning themselves to death in protest against the autocratic Diem regime in the mid 1960s. Few of you, however, know that Buddhist leaders worked throughout the war for a coalition government to rule the country more justly and ably, or that several Buddhist leaders experienced difficulties in their efforts to bring about reconciliation among the various factions within South Vietnam. Thich Nhat Hanh, one of the younger leading spokesmen for Vietnamese Buddhism during the war, spells out the goals of many Buddhists who worked for a more equitable political solution during the 1960s in a moving book, *Vietnam: Lotus in a Sea of Fire*. No American can read his appeal without feeling a deep sense of sadness over the lack of understanding of the Vietnamese situation shown by the United States.

In addition to the support Buddhist monks lent to nationalistic movements in the postcolonial era, Buddhism has also been used to fashion nationalistic political ideologies. U Nu, the former prime minister of Burma and a devout Buddhist, constructed a political ideology which he labeled Buddhist Socialism. The same slogan is being used by the Soka Gakkai movement in Japan. This Japanese "new" religion, a modern revival of a Buddhist sect of the thirteenth century, launched a political party a few years ago. Both U Nu and Daisetsu Ikeda of the Soka Gakkai argued that politics should serve humanitarian values and religious ideals. While U Nu was deposed as prime minister and the political party of the Soka Gakkai movement in Japan has had limited success, they provide contemporary examples of a tradition of interaction between Buddhism and politics beginning in the third century B.C.

Buddhist leaders throughout Asia have not been indifferent to the problems of the modern world. Meetings of the World Buddhist Association with representatives from all over Asia bear witness to the fact that Buddhists are profoundly concerned about political and social justice. On a practical level Buddhist monks in Thailand are enrolled in community development training programs in order to assist government officials in public health projects and in meeting rural needs such as sanitary wells, access roads, and schools. Monastic education on the university level in Sri Lanka and Thailand includes various secular subjects. In short, organized Buddhism is caught in the middle of the forces for political, economic, and social change. Buddhist monks have acted as articulate critics for political reform. Others have been instrumental in humanitarian programs aimed at social welfare and rural uplift. You are aware of the role religious spokespersons have played and continue to play in the fight for social and racial justice in the United States and of the many programs operated by churches and synagogues to meet particular needs in urban areas. Buddhists, as well as Christians and Jews, are concerned to alleviate human suffering.

People throughout the world face a very uncertain future marked by problems of increasing world population, food shortages, ecological imbalance, urban crises, redefinition of family patterns, and the breakdown of traditional values. Can religions like Buddhism provide any guidance? Indeed they can. On a sociological level they offer a stability through their particular world view and their ideas about people's place in that world view. Giving a sense of purpose and meaning to life in an unstable world is no mean achievement. In the area of values, Buddhism has consistently pointed out the fallacy in putting faith in materialism and secularism and has pointed to higher and more meaningful goals characterized by wisdom and equanimity. A quick glance at the newspaper headlines attests to the fact that heads of state and nations are sorely lacking either in wisdom or equanimity. These ideals are not unattainable abstractions available only to the holy man closeted away in a far-off temple. They are the inevitable consequence of a journey defined by moral virtue and mental training—a journey as available to you and me as to the monk. The Buddhist does not pretend that personal and social problems can be easily resolved, nor does he retreat from the world's suffering. Instead he tries to transform himself as the essential first step in the solution of broader social and political problems. Buddhism, with its strong emphasis on personal transformation, can contribute to the solution of these problems.

Notes

Part I: The Birth and Growth of Buddhism

1. From Henry Clarke Warren, *Buddhism in Translations* (Cambridge, Mass.: Harvard University Press, 1896; reissued by Atheneum Publishers, New York, 1962), pp. 46–47.

2. Adapted from Warren, op. cit., p. 53.

3. Adapted from Warren, op. cit., p. 61.

4. Buddhism has a vast and varied literature. It contains canonical texts originally divided into the categories of monastic discipline *(vanaya)*, teachings *(sutra)*, and higher philosophy *(abhidharma)*. Commentaries and subcommentaries were added and continue to be written. Buddhist literature also includes historical chronicles, legends and folk tales, poetry, sermons, and so on. Out of these extensive collections certain texts have become especially popular because they contain teachings that capture the essential meaning of a particular tradition. The *Dhammapada* would be such a text for the Theravada and the *Heart Sutra (Prajnaparamita Hrdaya)* for the Mahayana.

5. Much of our knowledge of the history of Theravada Buddhism in India and Sri Lanka comes from chronicles written by Sinhalese monks. The most famous are the *Mahavamsa,* the *Culavamsa,* and the *Dipavamsa.* Other Buddhist countries such as Burma and Thailand developed their own chronicle traditions.

Part II: The Teachings of Buddhism

1. Adapted from E. A. Burtt, ed., *The Teachings of the Compassionate Buddha* (New York: New American Library, Mentor Books, 1955), pp. 29–30.

2. For extensive textual references, see Edward Conze et al., *Buddhist Texts Through the Ages* (New York: Philosophical Library, 1954), pp. 65–82.

3. From the *Mahavagga,* I, 21. Adapted from E. J. Thomas, *Buddhist Scriptures* (London: John Murray, 1935), p. 54.

4. Translated by F. Max Muller, in *The Sacred Books of the East,* Vol. X, Pt. 1 (Oxford: Clarendon Press, 1899).

5. Adapted from Warren, op. cit., pp. 131–33.

6. From the *Majjhima-Nikaya,* 1, 428. Adapted from Warren, op. cit., pp. 120–21.

7. Adapted from translation by F. Max Muller, op. cit.

8. Walpola Rahula, *What the Buddha Taught* (New York: Grove Press, 1962), p. 35.

9. From *Path of Purity,* 507. Adapted from Conze et al., op cit., p. 100.

10. From *The Questions of King Milinda,* 268. Adapted from Conze et al., op. cit., p. 97.

11. From *Udana,* 81. Adapted from Conze et al., op. cit., pp. 94–95.

12. Adapted from translation by Shao Chang Lee, in *Popular Buddhism in China* (New York: Krishna Press, 1939), pp. 23–26.

13. From *Ashtasahasrika,* III, 58. Adapted from Conze et al., op. cit., pp. 143–44.

14. From *Sukhavativyuha,* Ch. 15. Adapted from Conze et al., op. cit., pp. 202–03.

15. From *Saddharmapundarika,* XXIV, vv. 17, 21–22. Adapted from Conze et al., op. cit., pp. 194–95.

Glossary

Amitabha, or Amitabha Buddha (also called "Amida" in Japan). One of the most popular visionary representations of Buddha, or images *not* patterned after the Indian Buddha Gautama or any other historical person. Called the Buddha of "immeasurable (a-mita) light (abha)," this Buddha is today the focus of devotion of the large Jodo and Shinshu sects in Japan.

an-atta. A Theravada concept that denies the existence of a soul or "self" beyond physical and mental attributes. Literally translated as "not self."

arahat. Theravada Buddhist saint. Literally translated as "worthy one."

bhikkhu. A homeless wanderer who is dependent on others for the necessities of life. A term applied to Buddhist monks.

bodhisattva. A Mahayana savior-saint—one who postpones the attainment of Nirvana in order to help others achieve that goal. Literally translated as "wisdom-being."

Brahmanism. The priestly, sacrificial religion of India which originated between 1500–2000 years prior to the Buddha and which became an important ingredient in Hinduism.

cetiya. A reliquary mound or shrine in which relics are kept.

Confucianism. A Chinese philosophy, based on the teachings of Confucius (551–479 B.C.), stressing devotion to parents and family, including the spirits of ancestors.

Dependent Co-origination. A twelve-stage cycle depicting life as an ongoing, ever-changing process.

Dhammapada. Famous Buddhist scriptures, compiler unknown, which were regarded by early Buddhists as utterances of the Indian founder Gautama. Considered a classic among the world's ethical literature. Translated as "scripture verses."

dharma. The teachings of the Buddha; the truth; the order of all things.

dukkha. Suffering rooted in desire and attachment.

Heart Sutra. One of the most important scriptures of the Zen sect of Mahayana Buddhism.

Hinduism. The philosophical, cultural, and social beliefs and practices that comprise the dominant religion in India. The world view is characterized by a belief in one supreme reality manifested in many forms as well as a belief in reincarnation.

Insight Meditation. The basic Buddhist meditative technique, the program for which is set out in the text *Foundation of Mindfulness*. The goal of practitioners is to achieve total awareness, which is believed to bring self-acceptance. Seated in a quiet place, with back straight, legs crossed, and eyes closed, meditators concentrate initially on their own breathing and then move to successively more difficult "meditation objects" like sensations, emotions, and ideas.

Jainism. An ascetic religion springing from Hinduism and founded in India by Makkali Gosala in the sixth century B.C. This sect stresses complete nonviolence and absolute protection of animals.

karma. A force, resulting from a person's actions during successive life cycles or reincarnations, that determines one's destiny in future reincarnations. Also, a type of yoga which seeks the highest self-realization through good deeds.

Mahayana. The form of Buddhism prevalent in China, Japan, Korea, and Vietnam. Literally translated as "the great vehicle."

Nichiren sect. A sect of Japanese Mahayana Buddhists founded by Saint Nichiren in the thirteenth century A.D.

Nirvana. A state of supreme bliss—the ultimate goal of Buddhism. Achievement of this goal releases one from the cycle of samsara. Literally translated as "a blowing out" or "extinction" of flame of desire or craving.

Pure Land. A Chinese and Japanese Buddhist sect emphasizing faith in the Buddha Amitabha (the Buddha of immeasurable light) and the goal of rebirth in his heaven of the Pure Land.

Rinzai. A contemporary sect of Japanese Zen Buddhism, practiced also at several Zen meditation centers in the United States.

sangha. The Buddhist community or monastic order. Literally translated as "group," "fellowship," or "community."

samsara. The cycle of birth, suffering, death, and rebirth. Literally translated as "a passing through."

Soka Gokkai. A modern revival of a thirteenth-century Buddhist sect which launched a political party in the 1960s. Characterizing its approach as "Buddhist Socialism," this party has a central philosophy that politics should serve humanitarian values and religious ideals.

Soto Zen sect. A contemporary sect of Japanese Zen Buddhism founded by Dogen in the thirteenth century.

sutra. A religious text or handbook summarizing the rudiments of a discipline or doctrine. Especially famous is the Yoga Sutra written by the Indian saint Patanjali, which gives the rudiments of the discipline of Yoga. Literally translated as "thread" and etymologically related to the English "suture."

Tantra (Tantrayana). A tradition within both Buddhism and Hinduism incorporating philosophical teachings as well as popular practices, sometimes referred to as magical and/or mystical. Emphasizes both male and female deities and is also well known for its elaborate rituals and disciplines. It became an important school of Buddhism in northern India from approximately the sixth century A.D. Also called Vajrayana.

Taoism. A Chinese philosophy and religion based on teachings of Lao-Tzu, sixth century B.C., as contained in the *Tao Te Ching*. This text teaches the supreme reality of the Tao (way) of nature, a dynamic interaction of opposites (yin and yang).

Theravada. The Buddhist school prevalent in Sri Lanka (called Ceylon before 1972), Burma, Thailand, Cambodia, and Laos. Literally translated as "Teachings of the Elders."

Transcendental Meditation. A non-Buddhist meditation technique specially adapted and marketed for Americans. It offers the easily learned method of mantra repetition for quieting the mind.

True Pure Land sect. A sect of the Pure Land tradition founded by Saint Shinran (thirteenth century) in Japan. Today it claims the greatest number of adherents of any Buddhist sect in Japan.

Vajrayana. A term used to characterize the Tantric tradition of Buddhism. Hence, Vajrayana and Tantrayana tend to be used interchangeably. Literally translated as "thunderbolt" or "diamond."

vinaya. The rules of discipline of the Buddhist monastic order.

Yoga. A discipline aimed at training the consciousness for a state of perfect spiritual insight and tranquility. Also, exercises done to promote control of the body and mind.

Zen, also Zen Buddhism. A Chinese and Japanese school of Mahayana Buddhism that asserts that enlightenment can be attained through meditation, self-contemplation, and intuition rather than through the scriptures.

Appendix

Buddhist Meditation Centers in the United States

There are dozens of Buddhist meditation centers throughout the United States. The teachers at some of these centers are Asians, but at others the teachers are American Buddhists trained in Asian countries. The following list is highly selective and indicates only a few of the centers where meditation is taught according to Zen, Tibetan, and Theravada methods.

The Buddhist Society
5184 Scranton Court
Denver, Colorado 80239

Gold Mountain Monastery
1731 15th
San Francisco, California 94103

Kwan Yin Temple
R.D. 2, Temple Road
Woodhull, New York 14898

Minnesota Zen Meditation Center
425 Fifth Street S.E.
Minneapolis, Minnesota 55414

San Francisco Zen Center
300 Page Street
San Francisco, California 94102

Shasta Abbey
R.R. 1, Box 577
Mount Shasta, California 96067

Tail of the Tiger
Star Route
Barnet, Vermont 05821

Tibetan Nyingma Meditation Center
2425 Hillside Avenue
Berkeley, California 94704

Vajrapani Institute for Wisdom and Culture
437 Altair Place
Venice, California 90291

Vipassana Fellowship of America
253 Lawrence Street
New Haven, Connecticut 06511

Zen Buddhist Temple
2230 North Halsted Street
Chicago, Illinois 60614

Zen Meditation Center of Rochester
7 Arnold Park
Rochester, New York 14607

Zen Studies Society, Inc.
223 East 67th Street
New York, New York 10021

Bibliography

Good books on Buddhism are now readily available in paperback. All general introductions to world religions—for example, Huston Smith, *The Religions of Man* (Harper & Row, 1965)—contain chapters on Buddhism. Buddhist publications are also available through the Buddhist Book Store, 1710 Octavia Street, San Francisco, California, the Washington Buddhist Vihara, Washington, D.C., and other Buddhist centers in most major cities in the country. Inexpensive pamphlets on a variety of Buddhist subjects including translations of Theravada texts are available through the Buddhist Publication Society, Kandy, Sri Lanka.

The following entries are highly selective and are annotated for easier use.

Bapat, P. V., ed. *2500 Years of Buddhism.* Mystic, Conn.: Lawrence Verry, 1971. A collection of articles on a wide variety of topics in the history and teaching of Buddhism. Quality and usefulness are uneven. Generally dry but informative.

Basham, Arthur L. *The Wonder That Was India.* 3rd ed. New York: Taplinger Publishing Co., 1968. An excellent introduction to the cultural history of India. Section on religion treats Buddhism.

Blofield, John. *The Tantric Mysticism of Tibet.* New York: E. P. Dutton & Co., 1970. A readable introduction to the Tantric Buddhism of Tibet.

————. *The Wheel of Life.* Berkeley, Calif.: Shambala Publications, 1972. An autobiographical account of an Englishman ordained into the Buddhist monkhood in China.

Burtt, E. A., ed. *The Teachings of the Compassionate Buddha.* New York: New American Library, Mentor Books, 1955. One of the standard anthologies of Buddhist texts containing generally well-known texts and translations.

Byles, Marie. *Journey into Burmese Silence.* London: George Allen & Unwin, 1962. A personal account of an Englishwoman's experience with meditation practice in Burma.

Campbell, Joseph. *The Hero with a Thousand Faces.* Rev. ed. Princeton, N.J.: Princeton University Press, 1968. A well-known scholar of myth and symbol argues for a common pattern to the biographies of a wide variety of gods and religious heroes including the Buddha.

Chang, Garma C. C. *The Practice of Zen.* New York: Harper & Row, 1970. A study of Zen thought including discourses on Zen practice and a survey of Buddhist meditation.

Ch'en, Kenneth K. S. *Buddhism: The Light of Asia.* Woodbury, N.Y.: Barron's Educational Series, 1968. The clearest, most straightforward introduction to the history of the development of Buddhism written by one of the foremost American scholars of Chinese Buddhism.

Conze, Edward. *Buddhism: Its Essence and Development.* New York: Harper & Row, 1959. One of the most widely used introductions to Buddhism. Stronger in the area of Buddhist thought than institutional Buddhism. Less readable than Ch'en, which is stronger in the area of institutional history.

_____, et al. *Buddhist Texts Through the Ages.* New York: Philosophical Library, 1954. Also published as a Harper & Row Torchbook, 1964. One of the standard collections of Buddhist texts with a wider ranging selection than Burtt or Hamilton. Arrangement is both by tradition and topic.

Coomaraswamy, Ananda K. *The Buddha and the Gospel of Buddhism.* New York: Harper & Row, 1964. Contains one of the most readily accessible accounts of the life of the Buddha.

Govinda, Lama A. *The Way of the White Clouds.* Berkeley, Calif.: Shambala Publications, 1971. An autobiographical sketch of a German Tantric Buddhist monk.

Hamilton, Clarence H., ed. *Buddhism: A Religion of Infinite Compassion.* Indianapolis: Bobbs-Merrill Co., 1952. One of the earliest paperback collections of selections from both Theravada and Mahayana Buddhist texts. Still useful.

Hanh, Thich Nhat. *Vietnam: Lotus in a Sea of Fire.* New York: Hill & Wang, 1967. An informative and moving account of the plight of Vietnam during the Indochina war and the role Buddhism sought to play in bringing peace to that country.

_____. *Zen Keys.* Translated by Jean and Albert Low. New York: Doubleday & Co., 1974. A variety of selections from Zen masters. Readable and enjoyable.

Herrigel, Eugene. *Zen in the Art of Archery.* New York: Random House, 1971. A Westerner's attempt to master one of the Zen martial arts. One of the best accounts of a first-hand encounter with the Zen mind.

Hesse, Hermann. *Siddhartha.* New York: New Directions Publishing Corp., 1951. A novel which uses themes from Buddhism.

Johnston, William. *Christian Zen.* New York: Harper & Row, 1974. Johnston, a Jesuit teaching in Japan, provides a sensitive Christian appreciation of Zen.

_____. *Silent Music.* New York: Harper & Row, 1974. A study of meditation employing both traditional Buddhist approaches as well as modern Western methods of analyzing the consequences of meditation techniques.

_____. *The Still Point.* New York: Harper & Row, 1971. A sympathetic look at Zen Buddhism by a Western Catholic living in Japan.

King, Winston L. *Buddhism and Christianity: Some Bridges of Understanding.* Greenwood, S.C.: Attic Press, 1962. This book came out of Professor King's two-year stay at the Institute of Advanced Buddhistic Studies in Rangoon, Burma. It is an examination of selected topics in the two traditions—for example, prayer and meditation—that are mutually enlightening to Christians and Buddhists.

_____. *In the Hope of Nibbana: The Ethics of Theravada Buddhism.* LaSalle, Ill.: Open Court Publishing Co., 1964. Few studies of Buddhist ethics are available. This book remains as one of the best of them.

_____. *A Thousand Lives Away.* Cambridge, Mass.: Harvard University Press, 1965. A lucid account of the varieties of Buddhism in Burma.

Lester, Robert C. *Theravada Buddhism in Southeast Asia.* Ann Arbor, Mich.: University of Michigan Press, 1973. One of the few surveys of Theravada Buddhism in Southeast Asia. Useful summary of Theravada doctrine.

Merton, Thomas. *The Asian Journals of Thomas Merton.* New York: New Directions Publishing Corp., 1975. Merton's journal was kept during his final visit to Asia where he spoke with many Asian religious leaders. It was published after his death and is his last written work. It shows his great sympathy with Asian spirituality.

_____. *Zen and the Birds of Appetite*. New York: New Directions Publishing Corp., 1968. This American Trappist monk's deep appreciation of Zen Buddhism has had a profound effect on the thinking of many Western Christians. This volume is a collection of essays on Buddhism and Christianity.

Morgan, Kenneth W., ed. *The Path of the Buddha*. New York: Ronald Press, 1956. A collection of essays by Asian Buddhists on a variety of aspects of Buddhist historical development and doctrine. Also includes selections from texts. Edited by the former head of Chapel House, Colgate University, whose contribution to the undergraduate study of Asian religions remains almost unmatched.

Nyanaponika, Thera. *The Heart of Buddhist Meditation*. New York: Citadel Press, 1969. A collection of Buddhist meditation texts with a study of insight meditation by the famous German monk, Thera Nyanaponika, of the Forest Hermitage, Kandy, Sri Lanka.

Pardue, Peter. *Buddhism: A Brief Account*. New York: Macmillan Co., 1971. An introduction to the social history of Buddhism. One of the few general introductions from a sociological point of view.

Pratt, James B. *The Pilgrimage of Buddhism and a Buddhist Pilgrimage*. New York: Macmillan Co., 1928. This classic study, long out of print, contains a mine of information about the history of Buddhism and Buddhist institutional life of the early twentieth century.

Rahula, Walpola. *What the Buddha Taught*. Rev. ed. New York: Grove Press, 1974. The best introduction to Theravada Buddhist thought by one of its foremost interpreters. The new edition also contains a selection of texts.

Reps, Paul, ed. *Zen Flesh, Zen Bones*. New York: Doubleday & Co., 1961. A useful and thoroughly delightful selection of sayings from Zen masters and other Zen texts. Contains the famous Ten Oxherding Pictures and selections from the *koan* collection known as the *Mumonkan* ("Gateless Gate").

Ross, Nancy, ed. *The World of Zen*. New York: Random House, 1960. This collection puts together a useful selection of essays on the Zen arts (e.g., gardens, painting, poetry) and other subjects.

Saddhatissa, H. *The Buddha's Way*. New York: George Braziller, 1972. Ranks next to Rahula as an introduction to Theravada thought. Like Rahula, the author is a Sinhalese monk.

Sato, Giei, and Eshin Nishimura. *Unsui: A Diary of Zen Monastic Life*. Honolulu: University Press of Hawaii, Eastwest Center Press, 1973. A delightful collection of watercolors about Zen monastic life by the monk, Sato, with commentary by Eshin Nishimura, head of the Zen Study Center, Hanazona Buddhist University, Kyoto, Japan.

Schecter, Jerrold. *The New Face of Buddha*. New York: Coward, McCann & Geohegan, 1967. A readable, popular treatment of the involvement of Buddhism in social and political change.

Suzuki, D. T. *An Introduction to Zen Buddhism*. New York: Ballantine Books, 1973. Suzuki has been the most celebrated interpreter of Zen Buddhism to the West. Of his many books on Zen, this slim volume treats the widest variety of subjects in the briefest scope.

Swearer, Donald K. *Buddhism in Transition*. Philadelphia: Westminster Press, 1970. This book focuses on Buddhism in contemporary Southeast Asia.

_____. *Secrets of the Lotus: Studies in Buddhist Meditation*. New York: Macmillan Co., 1971. Interpretations of meditation in the Theravada and Zen traditions. Also contains an account of a meditation workshop held at Oberlin College, Oberlin, Ohio.

Warren, Henry Clarke. *Buddhism in Translations*. Cambridge, Mass.: Harvard University Press, 1896. Reissued by Atheneum Publishers, 1962. An extensive collection of texts from the Theravada tradition.

Watts, Alan W. *The Way of Zen.* New York: Random House, Vintage Books, 1965. A readable interpretation of the historical development, teachings, and practice of Zen Buddhism by a well-known popularizer of Asian religions and philosophies.

————. *The Wisdom of Insecurity.* New York: Random House, Vintage Books, 1968. A provocative reinterpretation of the Buddhist notion of impermanence.

White, John, ed. *What Is Meditation?* New York: Doubleday & Co., 1974. Many studies of various kinds of meditation and their psychological and physiological effects are now available. This small book contains a number of essays by sympathetic interpreters of the importance of meditation practice.

Wray, Elizabeth, et al. *The Ten Lives of the Buddha.* New York: John Weatherhill, 1972. A beautiful collection of pictures from Thai temple paintings of the last ten Jataka tales (previous lives of the Buddha). Each Jataka story is outlined in some detail.